Sadlier WORD STUDY Reading

Level E

Senior Authors

Richard T. Vacca
Lesley Mandel Morrow

Contributing Authors

Charles T. Mangrum II, Ed.D.
Professor of Reading Education
University of Miami

Stephen S. Strichart, Ph.D.
Professor of Education
Florida International University

Program Consultants

Raymond P. Kettel, Ed.D.
Associate Professor of Education
University of Michigan
Dearborn, Michigan

Sylvia A. Rendón, Ph.D.
Coordinator for English Language Arts
Cypress-Fairbanks I.S.D.
Houston, Texas

Lisbeth Ceaser, Ph.D.
Dir., Precollegiate Academic Development
California Polytechnic State University
San Luis Obispo, California

Susan Stempleski, M.Ed., M.A.
Lecturer in TESOL
Teachers College, Columbia University
New York, New York

Sadlier-Oxford
A Division of William H. Sadlier, Inc.

Advisors

The publisher wishes to thank the following teachers and administrators who read portions of the series prior to publication for their comments and suggestions.

Rubbie D. Baker
Fifth Grade Teacher
Decatur, Georgia

Margarite K. Beniaris
Assistant Principal
Chicago, Illinois

Trish Bresch
Elementary School Teacher
Westmont, New Jersey

Carmen Talavera
Fourth Grade Teacher
Long Beach, California

Margaret Clifford
Principal
Michigan City, Indiana

Veronica Durden
Counselor
Beaumont, Texas

Christine Henschell
Sixth Grade Teacher
Grand Rapids, Michigan

Malini Horiuchi
Fifth Grade Teacher
Hollis Hills, New York

Amy T. Kwock
Principal
Honolulu, Hawaii

Connie Sartori
Sixth Grade L.A. Teacher
Seminole, Florida

Shaun R. Burke
Fourth Grade Teacher
Rancho Santa Margarita, California

Acknowledgments

William H. Sadlier, Inc., gratefully acknowledges the following for the use of copyrighted materials:

"Catching Up with Lewis and Clark" (text only). Reprinted from the October 10, 1997, issue of TIME FOR KIDS magazine, with the permission of the publisher, Time Inc. Copyright © 1997 Time Inc.

"Deep in the Heart of . . . Big Bend" (text only) by Bud McDonald. By permission of the author. Reprinted from FALCON magazine (March/April 1995), published by Falcon Press Publishing.

Dictionary pronunciation keys (text only). Reprinted from Macmillan School Dictionary 1, with the permission of the publisher, The McGraw-Hill Companies, Inc. Copyright © 1990 by Macmillan Publishing Company, a division of Macmillan, Inc.

"Digging Up the Past" (text only). Reprinted from the October 12, 1992, issue of TIME FOR KIDS magazine, with the permission of the publisher, Time Inc. Copyright © 1992 Time Inc.

"Fire in the Sky" (text only) by David Foster. By permission of the author. Reprinted from BOYS' LIFE magazine (February 1996), published by the Boy Scouts of America.

Adapted from "Hawaii: Then and Now" (text only) by Marcie Carroll. Copyright © 1995 with permission from OWL magazine, Bayard Presse Canada Inc.

"How to Grow a Painting" (text only) by Gail Skroback. Reprinted from 3*2*1 CONTACT; May 1996, © Sesame Workshop. All rights reserved.

"Native Peoples of the Northeast" (text only) by Trudie Lamb Richmond. Excerpted from COBBLESTONE's November 1994 issue: Indians of the Northeast Coast, © 1994, Cobblestone Publishing Company, 30 Grove Street, Suite C, Peterborough, NH 03458. All Rights Reserved. Reprinted by permission of the publisher.

"Rough, Tough Pecos Bill" (text only) by Lester David. By permission of Maggie Rosen. Reprinted from BOYS' LIFE magazine (October 1995), published by the Boy Scouts of America.

"Saving the Everglades" (text only). Reprinted from the October 1, 1999, issue of TIME FOR KIDS magazine, with the permission of the publisher, Time Inc. Copyright © 1999 Time Inc.

"Snowmobile Safari!" (text only) by W. E. Butterworth IV. By permission of the author and BOYS' LIFE magazine. Reprinted from BOYS' LIFE magazine (December 1995), published by the Boy Scouts of America.

Photo Credits: Aileen Ah-Tye: 168; Animals Animals/Gary Griffen: 77; Art Resource: 102; Artville/Burke & Triolo: 16 left & bottom right; California State Railroad Museum: 99; CORBIS/BETTMANN: The Mariners' Museum: 5 top; Peter Finger: 5 bottom center; Robert Holmes: 8, 189 background; Galen Rowell: 18; Richard T. Nowitz: 22, 113; Richard A. Cooke: 24, 91 top right, 191; Michael S. Yamashita: 25 inset, David J. & Janice L. Frent Collection: 28; BETTMANN: 29 top, 64, 65, 72 bottom right, 72 left, 73 top right, 81 inset, 131, 133 background, 134, 172, 166, 196, 216 left; Dave Bartruff: 29 bottom right; Richard Cummins: 29 right, 160; Kevin R. Morris: 32, 90, 139 bottom, 158; Bob Krist: 33, 211; CORBIS: 36 top left, 45, 86; 192 bottom right; David Muench: 39 background, 80, 91 bottom right, 108, 138, 198, 187, 194; Robert Landau: 43; Buddy Mays: 44, 93, 157, 197; Kevin Fleming: 48, 68; Terry Whittaker/Frank Lane Picture Agency: 50 top left; George McCarthy: 50 bottom right; Dave G. Houser: 58, 59 bottom right, 71 inset, 100, 122, 170 bottom right; Roger Ressmeyer: 59 top, 95, 96, 118, 139 top, 184; Craig Aurness: 59 bottom, 202; Tom Bean: 62, 91 top, 135, 136 left, 136 bottom right, 173 top, 185; Tim Thompson: 63, 105 inset; Jim Zuckerman: 67; Paul A. Souders: 71 background, 112; Philip Gould: 73 bottom right, 87, 139 bottom right; Layne Kennedy: 74, 110; Charles E. Rotkin: 75; Reuters NewMedia Inc.: 78; Phil Schermeister: 79, 167 inset, 173 bottom right; Ted Spiegel: 83; Joseph Sohn/ChromoSohn Inc.: 59 right, 85, 105 background, 117, 125, 183; Scott T. Smith: 91 bottom; Dewitt Jones: 97; Mark Gibson: 114; D. Boone: 115; Danny Lehman: 116, 133 inset; Catherine Karnow: 120; Marc Muench: 121; Morton Beebe, S.F.: 123; Andrew Brown/Ecoscene: 124; Jim Sugar Photography: 126; Liz Hymans: 128; Ansel Adams Publishing Rights Trust: 139 top right; Philip James Corwin: 141; Lowell Georgia: 143, 154; Ric Ergenbright: 146; Wolfgang Kaehler: 147, 179, 195; James Marshall: 148; James L. Amos: 155; Mark Garanger: 156; AFP: 163, 214; Roy Parkes/Eye Ubiquitous: 167 background; Raymond Gehman: 169; Neil Rabinowitz: 170 top left; Galen Rowell: 173 top center, 221; Rick Doyle: 173 top right, 181; Kelly-Mooney Photography: 173 bottom; Chase Swift: 176; Joel W. Rogers: 180; Steve Kaufman: 186, 215 background; Karl Weatherly: 188; Nik Wheeler: 189 inset, 216 bottom right; Roy Corral: 204; Nick Gunderson: 206; Owen Franken: 209; Kennan Ward: 215 inset; Bjorn Backe/Papilio: 222; B. Daemmrich/The Image Works: 82; Bob Daemmrich: 103; Eyewire: 36 bottom right; Michael Geissinger: 38; H. Armstrong Roberts, Inc./M. Berman: 13; H. Armstrong Roberts, Inc./ H. Armstrong Roberts: 25 background; Index Stock Imagery/Mark Hunt/PictureQuest: 52; Lady-Hawke Images/Dusty L. Perin: 27; Minden Pictures/Flip Nicklin: 177; National Gallery of Art/Alexander Calder: 88; National Park Service/Colonial National Historical Park: 55; Phil Degginger: 153; Photo Researchers, Inc./Steve Maslowski: 16 top right; Photo Resource Hawaii/Sal Moiraghi: 192 left; Photo Resource Hawaii/Joe Solem: 199; PhotoDisc: 56 bottom right; Photofest/RKO Radio Pictures, Inc.: 159; PICTUREQUEST: Michael W. Nelson/Stock South: 14; DigitalVision: 26 left, top left & bottom left; Jeff Greenberg/eStock Photography: 29 top right; Phyllis Picardi/Stock South: 35; Michael Newman/PhotoEdit: 37; Archive Photos: 39 inset; Lee Snider: 40; Ann Purcell/ Carl Purcell/Words & Pictures: 46; Canstock Images Inc./eStock Photography: 47; Erwin Bauer/Peggy Bauer/Bruce Coleman, Inc.: 49; Stockbyte: 56 top left; Siede Preis PhotoDisc: 81 background; David Burdett/Contact Press Images: 106; David Young-Wolf PhotoEdit: 161; Robert Fried/Stock, Boston: 178; Robert Schoen/Index Stock Imagery: 190; Alan Oddie/PhotoEdit: 213; Mark Kelly/Stock, Boston: 224; Richard L. Stack: 20; Robert Weldon: 149; Ron Kimball Photography, Inc.: 130; The Granger Collection: 152, 165; The Image Bank/Michael John O'Neill: 5; The Stock Market: 12; Bancroft Library, UC Berkeley: 145; Wayne Arnst/Great Falls Tribune: 162; Western Folklife Center: 150; © Wolfgang Kaehler 2000 www.wkaehlerphoto.com: 210.

Illustrators: Dirk Wunderlich: Cover; Cobblestone Magazine: 15; C. F. Payne: 119; Merle Nacht: 151; Function Thru Form: 16, 36, 49, 135, 144, 208, 217; Functional Art: Diane Ali, Batelman Illustration, Moffit Cecil, Adam Gordon, Susumu Kawabe, Larry Lee, John Quinn, Zina Saunders, Sintora Regina Vanderhorst, Michael Woo

Contents

A Symbol of Freedom

Every year millions of people take to the air or the road to visit the American land. Often, their first stop is one of the big cities in the Northeast. Sometimes, the Statue of Liberty is the first sight tourists see. This "mighty woman with a torch" stands in New York City as a symbol of freedom to the whole world.

Years ago, most immigrants to the United States got their first glimpse of the country when they sailed into New York Harbor. There, the best-known woman in the world welcomed them.

The Statue of Liberty was a present to the United States from the people of France. It marked the one hundredth birthday of our country. The project to build the statue took almost ten years to complete. At last, there was a grand ceremony on October 28, 1886. President Grover Cleveland was there. He said, "We will not forget that Liberty has here made her home...."

Millions of people visit the Statue of Liberty each year. Some choose to climb the 354 steps to her crown. At the top they can gaze at New York Harbor. From anywhere around the harbor, people can see the green statue and its golden torch. The torch stays lit all day and all night. It is a symbol of the light of liberty that shines on the American land.

Critical Thinking

1. What does the Statue of Liberty stand for?
2. How do you think immigrants felt when they first saw the Statue of Liberty?
3. How would you have felt? Explain to a partner.

Visit us at
www.sadlier-oxford.com

A Symbol of Freedom

UNIT 1
Northeast

Every year millions of people take to the air or the road to visit the American land. Often, their first stop is one of the big cities in the Northeast. Sometimes, the Statue of Liberty is the first sight tourists see. This "mighty woman with a torch" stands in New York City as a symbol of freedom to the whole world.

Years ago, most immigrants to the United States got their first glimpse of the country when they sailed into New York Harbor. There, the best-known woman in the world welcomed them.

The Statue of Liberty was a present to the United States from the people of France. It marked the one hundredth birthday of our country. The project to build the statue took almost ten years to complete. At last, there was a grand ceremony on October 28, 1886. President Grover Cleveland was there. He said, "We will not forget that Liberty has here made her home...."

Millions of people visit the Statue of Liberty each year. Some choose to climb the 354 steps to her crown. At the top they can gaze at New York Harbor. From anywhere around the harbor, people can see the green statue and its golden torch. The torch stays lit all day and all night. It is a symbol of the light of liberty that shines on the American land.

💡 Critical Thinking
1. What does the Statue of Liberty stand for?
2. How do you think immigrants felt when they first saw the Statue of Liberty?
3. How would you have felt? Explain to a partner.

LESSON 1: Introduction to Consonant Blends, Consonant Digraphs, and Double Consonant Sounds   **5**

Dear Family,

Welcome to Sadlier's *Word Study* program. Each unit presents strategies and exercises to help your child become a better reader. In Unit 1, your child will review and explore consonant blends, consonant digraphs, and double consonant sounds. The focus of Level E is the *American Land—Its People and History*. The unit theme is the *Northeast*.

A **consonant blend** is two or three consonants sounded together so that each letter is heard (**gl**ass, fie**ld**, **spl**inter).

A **consonant digraph** is two consonants that together stand for one sound (**ch**arm, wea**th**er, sa**sh**). The word digra**ph** itself ends with the digraph **ph,** which makes the sound of **f.**

The sound that **double consonants** make is usually the sound of just one of the consonants, as in ke**tt**le and ra**bb**it.

Family Focus

- Read together the nonfiction selection on page 5. Talk about it with your child. Discuss the meaning of a national symbol. What other symbols can your child identify? How do these symbols convey their meaning?

- Brainstorm places of national interest, such as Independence Hall, Plymouth Rock, or the White House. What historic places have you seen? Which historic landmarks do you hope to visit? Make a list of these places.

LINKS TO LEARNING

To extend learning together, you might explore:

Web Sites
www.nps.gov/stli/mainmenu.htm
www.libertystatepark.com/statueof.htm

Video
The Statue of Liberty, a film by Ken Burns, PBS Home Video.

Literature
Indians of the Northeast by Colin G. Calloway, ©1991.

Places to Visit
Plimouth Plantation, Plymouth, MA
The Statue of Liberty, New York, NY

Name _____

Helpful Hint

A **consonant blend** is two or three consonants sounded together so that each letter is heard. An **initial consonant blend** appears at the beginning of a word. Read these words with initial l-blends:

blanket   **cl**imate   **fl**ake   **gl**obe   **pl**ant   **sl**eep

★ **Fill in the circle of the blend that begins each picture name. Then write the initial l-blend on the line to complete the word.**

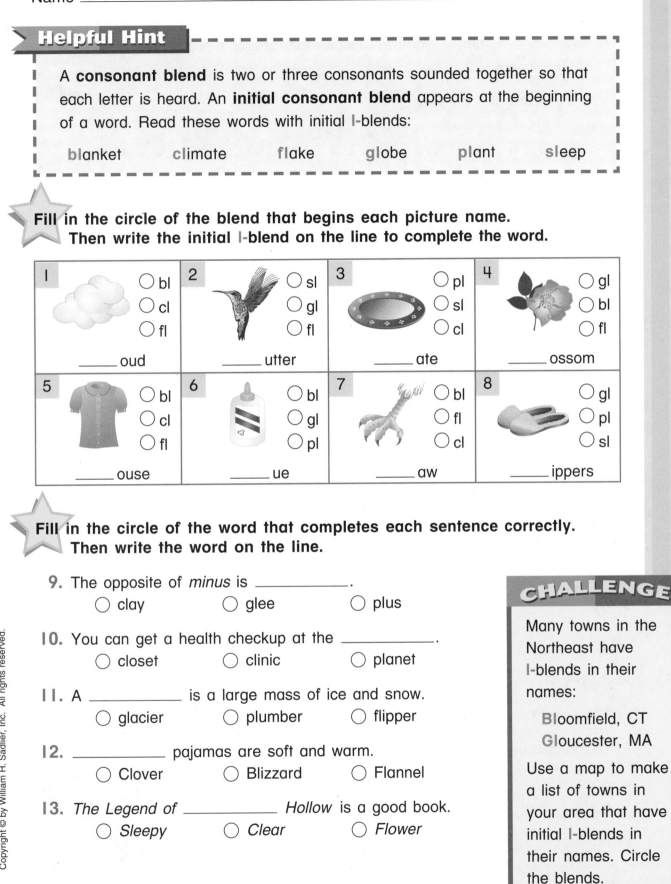

1. ○ bl ○ cl ○ fl   _____ oud

2. ○ sl ○ gl ○ fl   _____ utter

3. ○ pl ○ sl ○ cl   _____ ate

4. ○ gl ○ bl ○ fl   _____ ossom

5. ○ bl ○ cl ○ fl   _____ ouse

6. ○ bl ○ gl ○ pl   _____ ue

7. ○ bl ○ fl ○ cl   _____ aw

8. ○ gl ○ pl ○ sl   _____ ippers

★ **Fill in the circle of the word that completes each sentence correctly. Then write the word on the line.**

9. The opposite of *minus* is _____.
   ○ clay   ○ glee   ○ plus

10. You can get a health checkup at the _____.
   ○ closet   ○ clinic   ○ planet

11. A _____ is a large mass of ice and snow.
   ○ glacier   ○ plumber   ○ flipper

12. _____ pajamas are soft and warm.
   ○ Clover   ○ Blizzard   ○ Flannel

13. *The Legend of* _____ *Hollow* is a good book.
   ○ *Sleepy*   ○ *Clear*   ○ *Flower*

CHALLENGE

Many towns in the Northeast have l-blends in their names:

Bloomfield, CT
Gloucester, MA

Use a map to make a list of towns in your area that have initial l-blends in their names. Circle the blends.

A **phonogram** is a syllable that has a vowel and any letters that follow. Usually, a phonogram has a vowel followed by one or more consonants. Some phonograms have two vowels, but only one vowel sound.

Here are some phonograms:

ack   ance   ant   are   aw   ay   ide   ing   ink   ock   ug   ump

---

⭐ **Each box has three initial l-blends and three phonograms. Match the blends and the phonograms in each box to build three words. Write the words on the lines.**

1		2		3	
gl	ay	pl	ing	bl	ock
bl	ink	cl	are	gl	ump
pl	ide	gl	ug	sl	ance
_____		_____		_____	
_____		_____		_____	
_____		_____		_____	

⭐ **Write a word from the box below to complete each sentence about Gloucester, Massachusetts. This old town has a long history of fishing.**

block	claw	plant	play	black	glance

4. You can pick up a map of Gloucester at the tourist office,

   just one _____ from the port.

5. Sailors in _____ rubber boots slosh in water all day.

6. The largest docks lead to a major fish-processing _____.

7. The meat from a lobster _____ is very tasty.

8. A quick _____ toward the horizon shows that a storm is coming.

9. Actors performed a _____ about this fishing village.

Home Involvement Activity Find **Gloucester,** Massachusetts, on a map. Brainstorm ocean-related words that begin with an l-blend. **Fl**ounder is one. How many others can you name? Make a list.

Name _____

Helpful Hint

Many consonants blend with r. These words have initial r-blends:

bring   crumble   drain   frantic   ground   present   treat

Write an r-blend from the box below to complete each picture name.

| br | cr | dr | fr | gr | pr | tr |

1	2	3	4
_____ eckles	_____ ib	_____ iangle	_____ oceries
5	6	7	8
_____ occoli	_____ etzel	_____ apeze	_____ esser

Fill in the circle of the word that completes each sentence correctly. Then write the word on the line.

9. Wheat flour and corn meal are used in making _____.
   ○ brooks   ○ braids   ○ bread

10. A nightmare is a bad _____.
    ○ drain   ○ dream   ○ drummer

11. The winner gets to wear a glittery _____.
    ○ crash   ○ crown   ○ creature

12. The _____ backs up whenever the drawbridge opens.
    ○ trickle   ○ traffic   ○ trumpet

13. Get the _____ good and hot before you
    make pancakes.
    ○ greenhouse   ○ griddle   ○ gravy

CHALLENGE

Circle the r-blends in these words:

fresher
abroad
impress
grandfather

Then write a sentence for each word.

Helpful Hint

Many consonants blend with **s**. These words have initial **s**-blends:

score   **sk**ate   **sl**ip   **sp**oon   **st**ack   **sw**ing

⭐ **Each word in the box below has an initial s-blend. Choose the word from the box that names each picture. Then write the word on the line.**

scallop   **sk**eleton   **sl**icker   **sm**ile   **sn**orkel   **sp**inach   **st**amp   **sw**eater

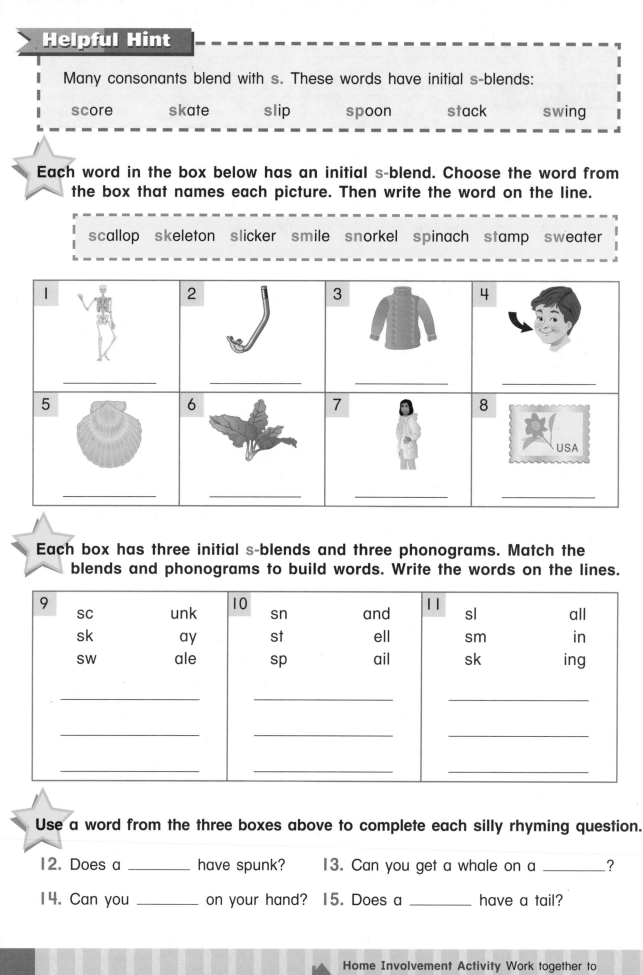

1	2	3	4
_____	_____	_____	_____

5	6	7	8
_____	_____	_____	_____

⭐ **Each box has three initial s-blends and three phonograms. Match the blends and phonograms to build words. Write the words on the lines.**

9		10		11	
sc	unk	sn	and	sl	all
sk	ay	st	ell	sm	in
sw	ale	sp	ail	sk	ing
_____		_____		_____	
_____		_____		_____	
_____		_____		_____	

⭐ **Use a word from the three boxes above to complete each silly rhyming question.**

12. Does a _____ have spunk?   13. Can you get a whale on a _____?

14. Can you _____ on your hand?   15. Does a _____ have a tail?

10   LESSON 3: Initial **r**- and **s**-blends

Home Involvement Activity Work together to list items in your home that begin with **r**-blends and **s**-blends, such as **br**oom and **st**airs. Circle the **r**- and **s**-blends in the words on your list.

Name _____

Helpful Hint

A **final consonant blend** appears at the end of a word.

be**lt**   fie**ld**   hi**nt**   ju**mp**   le**ft**   li**sp**   pu**lp**   re**st**   soun**d**

⭐ **Say** the name of each picture. Listen for the final blend. Then circle the blend that ends each picture name. Write that blend on the line to complete the word.

1 nt lt st pai____	2 ld nt st li____	3 lt ld nd me____	4 mp sp ft ra____
5 mp nt ld fo____	6 nd ft sp grou____	7 nd lp mp lu____	8 nt sp nd wa____

⭐ **Which word in each pair has a final consonant blend? Circle the word.**

9. Provide *or* pretend

10. Small *or* scalp

11. Stump *or* stupid

12. Grasp *or* great

⭐ **Write a word from the box below to complete each sentence.**

> hold   Coast   lift   surround

13. Newark, New Jersey, has the largest port on

the East _____.

14. Two great cargo terminals _____ Newark Bay.

15. Tall cranes _____ giant containers of goods.

16. The warehouses _____ many goods.

WORK TOGETHER

Another final consonant blend is **rt**, as in po**rt**. Work with a partner. List as many words as you can that end in **rt**.

LESSON 4: Final **t-**, **d-**, and **p-** blends   11

Some words have an **initial consonant blend** *and* a **final consonant blend**.

blast   crisp   draft   grind   plant   scold   slurp   sport   stamp   trend

⭐ **Underline the initial and final consonant blends in each word in bold type.**

1. White-water rafting requires **swift** water.

2. The campers pounded in the stakes with a **blunt** rock.

3. The members of the hiking club have **trust** in their leader.

4. **Grasp** the handle and turn it to the right.

5. Hot milk can **scald** you.

6. The story is set in the **present** time.

7. That is a well-known **brand** of cranberry sauce.

8. To fold the table, you must loosen the **clamp.**

9. I can daydream for hours as the clouds **drift** by.

10. They started a fire with sparks from a piece of **flint.**

⭐ **Say each word in the list. Listen for initial and final consonant blends. On the line, write the letter of the word from the list that matches each clue. Then underline the initial and final consonant blends in each word in the list.**

_____ 11. the opposite of *back*   **a.** blond

_____ 12. the opposite of *stop*   **b.** front

_____ 13. to make believe   **c.** grand

_____ 14. a sharp pain in a muscle   **d.** plump

_____ 15. large or excellent   **e.** pretend

_____ 16. chubby, like a baby   **f.** cramp

_____ 17. light yellow hair   **g.** draft

_____ 18. a current of air   **h.** start

Home Involvement Activity Work together to list words that rhyme with these words: **graft, blend,** and **clamp.** Try to find at least three rhymes for each word.

Name _____

> ### Helpful Hints

A **consonant digraph** is two consonants that together stand for one sound.

Initial digraphs *begin* words.   charm   phone   shelf   thin   whale

Medial digraphs are *in the middle* of words.   merchant   telephone   author

Final digraphs *end* words.   touch   sing   graph   rush   path

Read each group of words. Circle the consonant digraph in the word in bold type. Then write I for Initial, M for Medial, or F for Final, depending on where the consonant digraph appears in the word.

1. **rang** the alarm _____

2. heard the **whistle** _____

3. snapped a **photo** _____

4. **establish** the rules _____

5. sat in the **bleachers** _____

6. saw **another** fire _____

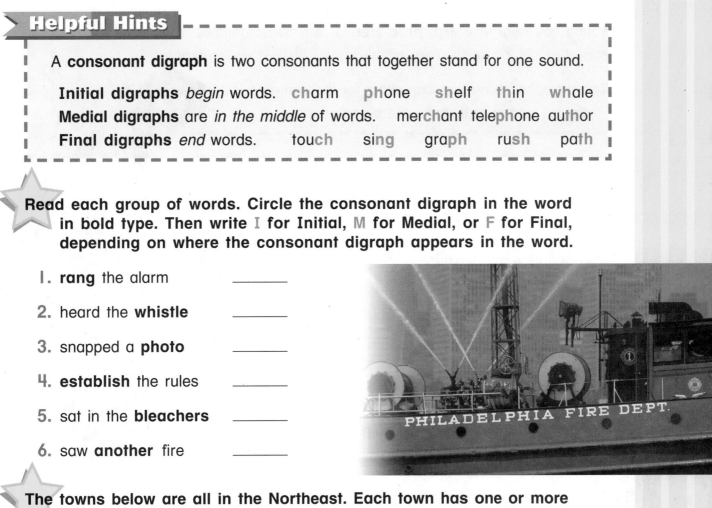

PHILADELPHIA FIRE DEPT.

The towns below are all in the Northeast. Each town has one or more consonant digraphs in its name. Circle the letter I for Initial, M for Medial, or F for Final to show where in the name each digraph appears. Then add the number of digraphs in each name.

Name of Town	Location of Digraph(s)			Number of Digraphs
7. Sharpsburg, MD	I	M	F	_____
8. Philadelphia, PA	I	M	F	_____
9. Chepachet, RI	I	M	F	_____
10. Moonachie, NJ	I	M	F	_____
11. Portsmouth, NH	I	M	F	_____
12. Cheshire, MA	I	M	F	_____

> ### CHALLENGE

Choose a state in the Northeast. Use a map to list place names in the state that have one or more consonant digraphs. Add the total number of consonant digraphs in the names.

Helpful Hints

The **digraph ch** can make three different sounds. Usually, it makes the sound you hear in **chirp, preacher,** or **birch.** Sometimes, it makes the sound of **sh,** as in **chiffon,** or the sound of **k,** as in **character.**

The digraphs **ph** and **gh** can stand for the same sound. **Physical** and **rough** make the same sound of **f.**

⭐ **Each word in the box below has the consonant digraph ch, ph, or gh. Write the word on the line that best completes each sentence.**

| telephone | rough | Chesapeake |

1. Maryland's _____ Bay is famous for its crabs.

2. There is a stretch of _____ road near Woodstock, New York.

3. We used our cellular _____ to say we'd be arriving in Boston soon.

Catching crabs on **Ch**esapeake Bay

⭐ **Each of the scrambled words below has a consonant digraph. Use the clues in each sentence to unscramble the word. Then write the letters in the spaces. The boxes show where the digraphs belong.**

4. I got a **fwifh** of salt air crossing the bridge to Cape Cod.
☐☐ _ _ _

5. Although there are snakes in the Northeast, there are no **tpynosh.**
_ _ ☐☐ _ _ _

6. We could smell that **meclhcai** spill on the road.
☐☐ _ _ _ _ _ _

7. Several **llfhsiyje** washed up on the beach after the storm.
_ _ _ _ _ _ _ ☐☐

8. It takes a lot of **scilyhap** effort to hike through Bear Mountain.
☐☐ _ _ _ _ _ _

9. Many houses in the Northeast are **tatahced** to each other.
_ _ _ _ ☐☐ _ _

Home Involvement Activity Together, look at a road atlas. Which main highways crisscross the Northeast? Which are north-south roads? Which roads go east-west? Which might you take to go up the coast?

LESSON 5: Consonant Digraphs

Name _____

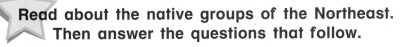

⭐ **Read about the native groups of the Northeast.
Then answer the questions that follow.**

Native Peoples of the Northeast

by Trudie Lamb Richmond

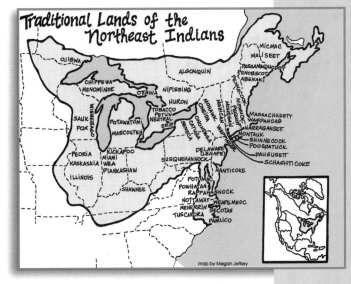

Traditional Lands of the Northeast Indians

map by Megan Jeffery

The Northeast is often defined as the area stretching from the Great Lakes region east to the Atlantic coast and from southern Canada and Maine south through Pennsylvania to the Tidewater region of Virginia. It is a broad and diverse area in both landscape and climate. Seasons range from harsh winters and cool summers in the north to milder winters and hot, humid summers in the south.

Five hundred years ago, when the first European explorers arrived, they discovered that the area was occupied by the Iroquois and the Algonquians. Within these two groups, there were many different tribes, bands, and villages, each with its own language and way of life. Most native groups in the Northeast grew some food and did not depend solely on hunting and gathering.

All the groups had a deep respect for the land and the plant and animal life they depended on. Hunting, for example, was never done for sport. Aside from food, animals were a valuable source of clothing, shelter, and tools.

There are an estimated 157,000 native people living in the Northeast of the United States today. Penobscots, Micmacs, Pequots, Wampanoags, Abenakis, Narragansetts, Mohawks, Mohegans, and others live in cities, towns, and rural areas, as well as on reservation lands set aside for their ancestors long ago.

📖 Reader's Response

1. **Who are some of the native peoples of the Northeast?**

2. **What do you think life was like for these people before the European explorers arrived? After the explorers came?**

3. **Why do you think these native groups respect the land and its plants and animals? Give reasons.**

For thousands of years, Native Americans of the Northeast have lived in harmony with the land. In what ways have these people respected nature? How is their treatment of the earth different from the way some people treat the environment today?

Imagine that you are a hawk looking down at our damaged environment. You might see trees being chopped down or people polluting the air or the water. How would these sights make you feel? Write a poem from the hawk's point of view. Then tell what people can do to help the earth survive. Use at least two of these words in your poem.

environment   nature   glance   chance   coast   path   survive
pollution   solution   pleasure   treasure   gather   respect   future

Writer's Tips

- Before writing, imagine the scene of a damaged environment that you could use in your poem. What might the hawk see?

- Remember that you are telling your poem from the hawk's point of view.

Speaker's Challenge

Practice reading your poem with a small group. If your poem is serious, be sure to use a serious tone of voice. Then give a choral reading of your poem to another group. Use expression and feeling.

Name _____

Fill in the circle of the blend or digraph that completes each picture name. Then write the blend or digraph on the line to complete the word.

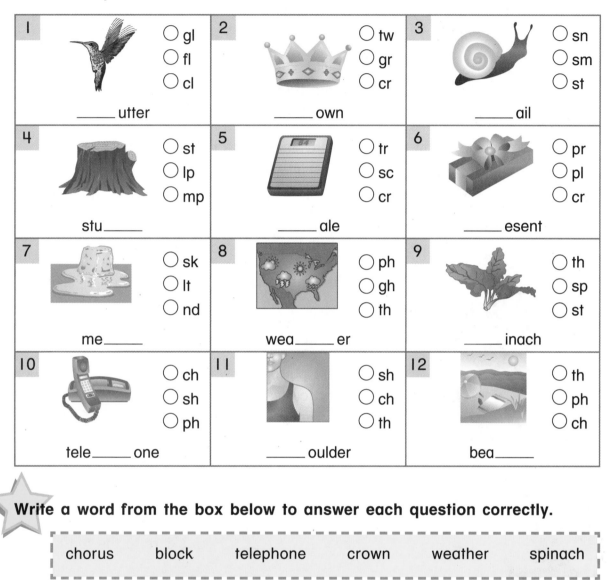

1	○ gl ○ fl ○ cl	_____ utter
2	○ tw ○ gr ○ cr	_____ own
3	○ sn ○ sm ○ st	_____ ail
4	○ st ○ lp ○ mp	stu _____
5	○ tr ○ sc ○ cr	_____ ale
6	○ pr ○ pl ○ cr	_____ esent
7	○ sk ○ lt ○ nd	me _____
8	○ ph ○ gh ○ th	wea _____ er
9	○ th ○ sp ○ st	_____ inach
10	○ ch ○ sh ○ ph	tele _____ one
11	○ sh ○ ch ○ th	_____ oulder
12	○ th ○ ph ○ ch	bea _____

Write a word from the box below to answer each question correctly.

chorus   block   telephone   crown   weather   spinach

13. Which can be cloudy or sunny? _____

14. Which is a group of singers? _____

15. Which do you speak into? _____

16. Which is worn by a king or a queen? _____

17. Which is a vegetable? _____

18. Which is another name for *street*? _____

Read the sentences. Fill in the circle of the word that correctly completes each sentence. Then write the word on the line.

1. Have you heard of Lake Placid, in New York _____?
   ○ South   ○ Coast   ○ State

2. In 1980, the Winter Olympic Games took place _____.
   ○ first   ○ there   ○ when

3. Visitors to Lake Placid can still see the ski _____, the hockey stadium, and other places built for the Olympics.
   ○ jumps   ○ pumps   ○ clumps

4. No one who saw the Olympic Games there can forget the _____ of the U.S. hockey team over the team from the Soviet Union.
   ○ touch   ○ triumph   ○ physical

5. Athletes who live in cold _____ take part in many winter sports.
   ○ crescents   ○ shoulders   ○ climates

6. Some people like to play ice hockey or skate on a _____ pond in the winter.
   ○ frozen   ○ shoulders   ○ stolen

7. Others put on snowshoes to _____ through wintry forests.
   ○ jump   ○ trudge   ○ bump

8. Still others cross-country ski over open _____.
   ○ feasts   ○ plants   ○ fields

9. The Northeast is famous for skiing. Ski centers have _____ to get skiers to the top of the runs.
   ○ lifts   ○ gifts   ○ drifts

U.S. vs. the Soviet Union—1980
Winter Olympics, Lake Placid, NY

Extend & Apply

Think of a different winter word for each clue. Write the word on the line.

10. It has an initial blend. _____
11. It has a final blend. _____
12. It has an initial digraph. _____
13. It has a final digraph. _____

Name _____

Helpful Hint

Some consonant blends or digraphs are made up of three letters. You will find **three-letter consonant blends** in words such as **scr**amble.

Here are some three-letter blends:

chr   sch   scr   shr   spl   spr   str   thr

⭐ **Write one of the three-letter blends from the box above to complete each sentence.**

1. The train whistle makes a high, _____ill sound.

2. The actors study the _____ipt to learn their lines.

3. Fenders on old cars used to be made of shiny

   _____ome.

4. Founded in 1635, Boston Latin is the oldest _____ool in the United States.

5. The season between winter and summer is _____ing.

WORK TOGETHER

You know that **u** is not a consonant. Yet sometimes, **squ** is called a three-letter consonant blend.

Get together with a small group. List words, such as **squ**irrel, that have the **squ**-blend.

⭐ **Unscramble the letters to name the picture. Then write the name of the picture on the line.**

6	7	8
buhrs	norhet	cwers
_____	_____	_____

9	10	11
sphals	inrestar	cloosh
_____	_____	_____

Use a word from the box to solve each clue. Write one letter in each space. Then read down the shaded column to answer the question below.

> Christina   scheme   schooner   scrambled   scroll   shriek
> shrug   splint   spread   straddle   straight   thrifty   throb

1. a type of cooked eggs   _ _ _ _ _ _ _ _ _

2. a ship with many masts and sails   _ _ _ _ _ _ _ _

3. once, a queen of Sweden   _ _ _ _ _ _ _ _ _

4. to pound, like a heart   _ _ _ _ _

5. a thin support to keep a broken bone in place   _ _ _ _ _ _

6. a secret or dishonest plan   _ _ _ _ _ _

7. the opposite of *crooked*   _ _ _ _ _ _ _ _

8. being careful about spending money   _ _ _ _ _ _ _

9. a loud, sharp yell or scream   _ _ _ _ _ _

10. to stand or sit with one leg or foot on either side   _ _ _ _ _ _ _ _

11. to open or stretch out   _ _ _ _ _ _

12. a long piece of paper you read by unrolling it   _ _ _ _ _ _

13. shoulder motion that means you don't know or care   _ _ _ _ _

Question: Josh the Wonder Dog was a mutt who lived in Glen Burnie, Maryland. Before he died in 1977, 478,802 people helped him earn an amazing record. What was it?

Answer: Josh was the world's _____

_____.

Josh the Wonder Dog

Home Involvement Activity Find out about these Northeastern cities that begin with three-letter consonant blends: Scranton, PA; Spring Lake, NJ; Stratford, CT. Write a brief fact sheet for each city.

Name _____

Helpful Hint

Double consonants often make one sound. You hear only one sound of **p** in **ripple.** You hear only one sound of **m** in **grammar.** You hear only one sound of **b** in **bubble.**

⭐ **Say** the name of each picture. Then fill in the missing double consonant to complete the word.

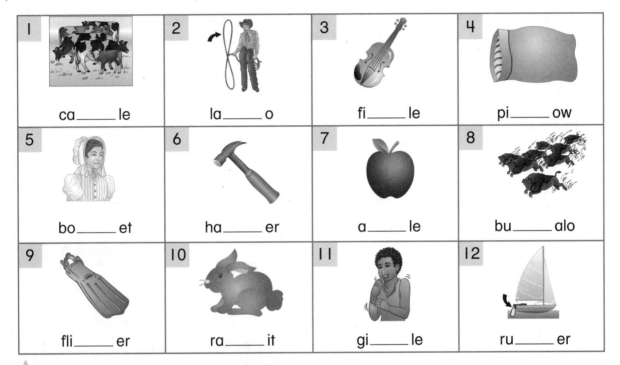

1 ca_____le	2 la_____o	3 fi_____le	4 pi_____ow
5 bo_____et	6 ha_____er	7 a_____le	8 bu_____alo
9 fli_____er	10 ra_____it	11 gi_____le	12 ru_____er

⭐ **Each word in the box below has a double consonant. Write a word from the box to complete each sentence.**

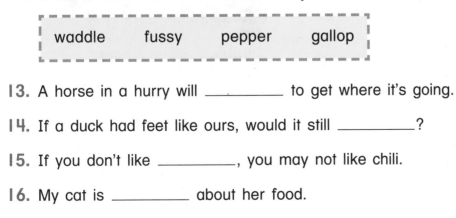

> waddle   fussy   pepper   gallop

13. A horse in a hurry will _____ to get where it's going.

14. If a duck had feet like ours, would it still _____?

15. If you don't like _____, you may not like chili.

16. My cat is _____ about her food.

WORD STRATEGY

When do you double a consonant? Listen to the vowel sound that comes before a double consonant. For example, the vowel **i** has a *long* sound in **diner** but a *short* sound in **dinner.** Write a spelling rule for double consonants.

There are some exceptions to the sound that double consonants make.

In some words spelled with a double **c**, the first **c** has the sound of **k**, as in **k**ite, and the second **c** has the sound of **s**, as in **s**ail.

accept = ak/**s**ept   **accident** = ak/**s**ident

Here is an exception for double **g**: In **sugg**est, most Americans pronounce the first **g** as the **g** in **g**o and the second **g** as **j**, as in **j**et.

Read the sentences. Underline each word that has a double c. Then read each underlined word aloud. Sort the words by the sound that the double c makes. Write the words correctly in the chart below.

1. Our class trip to Washington, DC, was a special occasion.

2. Two parents accompanied our class on the trip.

3. At one museum, we accepted free passes.

4. Our guide there was eccentric. He walked back and forth the whole time.

5. He was funny, too. He could speak with different accents.

6. The information he gave us was both interesting and accurate.

7. All the museums we visited had wheelchair access.

8. There was plenty to occupy us at the Air and Space Museum.

9. All in all, the trip was a great success.

10. We accomplished all we had set out to do.

Double c as in *accordion*	Double c as in *accept*

Home Involvement Activity Look together at the words with double c in the chart. Add at least two more words to each column.

Name _____

Some words have **irregular double consonant sounds.** These are two different consonants that together make one sound. One letter in the pair is silent.

The consonants **gn** and **kn** sound like **n**, as in **gn**at, **kn**it, and de**sign**.

lm sounds like **m** → ca**lm**   **sc** sounds like **s** → **sc**ene

mb sounds like **m** → cli**mb**   **wr** sounds like **r** → **wr**ite

The consonants **dg** together sound like **j**, as in bri**dg**e.

Say the name of each picture. Then fill in the two missing consonants to complete the word.

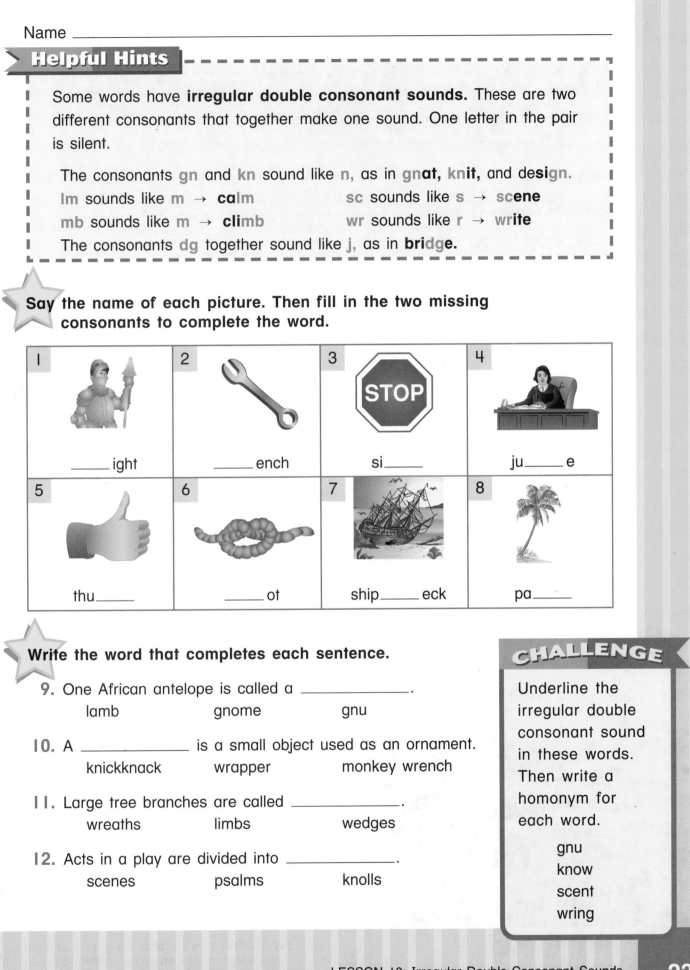

1	2	3	4
_____ight	_____ench	si_____	ju_____e
5	6	7	8
thu_____	_____ot	ship_____eck	pa_____

Write the word that completes each sentence.

9. One African antelope is called a _____.
   lamb   gnome   gnu

10. A _____ is a small object used as an ornament.
    knickknack   wrapper   monkey wrench

11. Large tree branches are called _____.
    wreaths   limbs   wedges

12. Acts in a play are divided into _____.
    scenes   psalms   knolls

CHALLENGE

Underline the irregular double consonant sound in these words. Then write a homonym for each word.

gnu
know
scent
wring

Use a word from the box to solve each clue. Write one letter in each space. Then read down the shaded column to answer the question below.

thumb	wreath	rewrite	assign	fudge	hedge	wrinkle	align
knoll	grudge	wriggle	crumb	knapsack	knob	lamb	scenery

1. a soft candy   _ _ _ _ _

2. to write something again   _ _ _ _ _ _ _

3. to put in a straight line   _ _ _ _ _

4. a small, rounded hill   _ _ _ _ _

5. a canvas bag   _ _ _ _ _ _ _ _

6. a young sheep   _ _ _ _

7. a small fold in paper   _ _ _ _ _ _ _

8. handle on a door   _ _ _ _

9. backdrop on a stage   _ _ _ _ _ _ _

10. a long-held dislike or anger   _ _ _ _ _ _

11. twist from side to side   _ _ _ _ _ _ _

12. a tiny piece of cake or bread   _ _ _ _ _

13. to give something as a task   _ _ _ _ _ _

14. a row of shrubs or trees   _ _ _ _ _

15. flowers woven together   _ _ _ _ _ _

16. your shortest digit   _ _ _ _ _

Question: The house in the photograph is called Fallingwater. It is in Pennsylvania. What famous architect built it?

Answer: _____.

LESSON 10: Irregular Double Consonant Sounds

 Home Involvement Activity What are some interesting or unusual buildings in your city or town? Make a list together. Describe what makes them special. Pay a visit to one, if possible.

Name _____

⭐ **Read each group of words. Say and spell each word in bold type. Repeat the word. Then sort the words by their initial consonant blend or digraph. Write each word in the correct column below.**

- a **cluster** of trees

- two **thumbs** up

- a pie **graph**

- **frequent** visitors

- cherry **blossoms**

- gave **specific** directions

- clouds **drifting** by

- at the **present** time

- **pleasing** scenery

- gave a **thorough** report

- **physical** fitness

- leafy **broccoli**

- **trudge** through snow

- fit into our **schedule**

- **flutter** its wings

- prize-winning **photographer**

- caught a quick **glimpse**

- a **splashing** sound

Niagara Falls, New York

A–F	G–R	S–Z

If you want tourist information about a state, you're in luck. Every state has a tourist office that sends free information to people who ask for it. Most almanacs list the office's address, telephone number, and Web site.

Choose a place in the Northeast that you would like to visit. Write a business letter to the state's tourist office. Ask for maps and other tourist information. Say what you want to see. Use at least two of these spelling words. Have your teacher help you mail your letter.

cluster	thumbs	graph	frequent	blossoms	specific
drifting	present	pleasing	thorough	physical	broccoli
trudge	schedule	flutter	photographer	glimpse	splashing

_____ Your Address

_____

_____ Date

Inside Address **Tourist Office of**_____

_____

_____

Greeting **To Whom It May Concern:**

Body _____

_____

_____

_____

Sincerely,   Closing

_____   Signature

Writer's Tip

Use letter parts correctly. Include your address, the date, the office to whom you are writing, a greeting, a closing, and your signature.

Speaker's Challenge

Get together with a classmate. Role-play a telephone conversation between you and a person who works in a tourist office. Write some of your questions beforehand.

Name _____

Read each sentence. Listen for the sound that the underlined letters make. Then circle *two* other words in the sentence that contain the same sound.

1. Nathan <u>kn</u>ows not to race that horse.

2. Please si<u>gn</u> your name on the dotted line.

3. Mr. Jackson had an a<u>cc</u>ident with that axe.

4. The denti<u>st</u> was still there yesterday.

5. General Daley ple<u>dg</u>ed justice for all.

6. Carl put the <u>ch</u>emistry set in the kitchen.

7. Mother's locket fits into the pa<u>lm</u> of my hand.

8. Doing the dog pa<u>dd</u>le helps us to swim.

9. I may never have a name for my <u>gn</u>u!

10. It never o<u>cc</u>urred to me that Kent could ride.

11. Rob noticed a <u>wr</u>inkle in the title page of the report.

12. The tele<u>ph</u>one rang five times before nine o'clock.

13. <u>Ch</u>ris knows that Mr. Krauss likes chocolate ice cream.

14. A few rou<u>gh</u> games caused physical problems.

15. Marcy, don't put your thu<u>mb</u> in your mouth!

Write a word from the box to complete each sentence correctly.

┌───┐
│ calm   gallop   grudge   knob   │
└───┘

16. Listen to the rhythmic sound when horses _____ at top speed.

17. He tried to open the door, but the _____ refused to budge.

18. I swim in the ocean only when the water is _____.

19. Can your brother really hold a _____ for a whole week?

Read about everyone's favorite uncle. Then fill in the circle of the word below that completes the sentence.

You've probably seen Uncle Sam. He's that **1** white-haired man in red, white, and blue clothes and a top hat. Uncle Sam is a symbol of the United States. But did you know that there really was an Uncle Sam? He was Sam Wilson of Arlington, Massachusetts.

In 1789, Sam Wilson moved to Troy, New York. There, he opened a meat-packing business. He was <u>well liked</u> by his **2**. They soon gave him the friendly nickname of "Uncle Sam." Wilson had a contract to sell meat to the United States Army. His workers stamped certain crates with the letters *U.S.*, which stood for *United States*. Rumor has it that workers joked about those letters. They said that they stood for their boss, **U**ncle **S**am. The joke spread. Over time, Uncle Sam came to stand for the American **3**. The real Sam Wilson died in 1854. He is buried in Troy, New York. If you visit that city you can pay your **4** to the real Uncle Sam.

1. ○ plump   ○ accurate   ○ skinny   ○ shrinking

2. ○ authors   ○ owners   ○ opponents   ○ customers

3. ○ preacher   ○ character   ○ chorus   ○ branch

4. ○ respects   ○ trust   ○ samples   ○ share

Reread the passage. Circle the letter of the correct answer.

5. Why did people call Sam Wilson "Uncle Sam"?
   a. He was a soldier.
   b. They had warm feelings for him.
   c. He was their uncle.
   d. He had many nieces.

6. What does it mean to say that Sam was <u>well liked</u>?
   a. He was liked by a few people.
   b. People were jealous of him.
   c. Everyone respected him.
   d. People enjoyed being with him.

Extend & Apply

Imagine that you are planning to go to a costume party dressed as Uncle Sam. What will you wear? How will you act? Write a description.

Making History in the Southeast

The Southeast region of the United States is filled with history. For example, in 1607, Jamestown, Virginia, became the first permanent English settlement. Almost 300 years later, Kitty Hawk, North Carolina, became the scene of an event that would change history.

When Wilbur and Orville Wright were boys, their father taught them to think for themselves. In fact, he encouraged them to explore anything that sparked their interest. As a result, Wilbur and Orville Wright began building things that might fly.

First, they built a kite. Next, they built a glider. Then, they built an airplane. The brothers named the plane *Flyer*. They took the *Flyer* to Kitty Hawk, North Carolina. Kitty Hawk is a vast open space on North Carolina's Outer Banks. There, on December 17, 1903, the Wright Brothers made the world's first flight by a motor-powered airplane. On the first try, the *Flyer* stayed in the air for all of 12 seconds! Later that day, the *Flyer* stayed up for 59 seconds. It covered a distance nearly as long as three football fields.

Today, you can see a full-sized model of the *Flyer* at Kitty Hawk. On December 17 of each year, you can also attend a ceremony to honor the flight of Wilbur and Orville Wright.

Critical Thinking

1. What happened in Kitty Hawk, North Carolina, on December 17, 1903?

2. How did the flight of the Wright Brothers change the way people live today?

3. Are you like Wilbur and Orville Wright? Are you interested in new ideas? Do you like to build things? Explain.

Word Study at Home

Dear Family,

UNIT 2
Southeast

Making History in the Southeast

The Southeast region of the United States is filled with history. For example, in 1607, Jamestown, Virginia, became the first permanent English settlement. Almost 300 years later, Kitty Hawk, North Carolina, became the scene of an event that would change history.

When Wilbur and Orville Wright were boys, their father taught them to think for themselves. In fact, he encouraged them to explore anything that sparked their interest. As a result, Wilbur and Orville Wright began building things that might fly.

First, they built a kite. Next, they built a glider. Then, they built an airplane. The brothers named the plane *Flyer*. They took the *Flyer* to Kitty Hawk, North Carolina. Kitty Hawk is a vast open space on North Carolina's Outer Banks. There, on December 17, 1903, the Wright Brothers made the world's first flight by a motor-powered airplane. On the first try, the *Flyer* stayed in the air for all of 12 seconds! Later that day, the *Flyer* stayed up for 59 seconds. It covered a distance nearly as long as three football fields.

Today, you can see a full-sized model of the *Flyer* at Kitty Hawk. On December 17 of each year, you can also attend a ceremony to honor the flight of Wilbur and Orville Wright.

Critical Thinking

1. What happened in Kitty Hawk, North Carolina, on December 17, 1903?
2. How did the flight of the Wright Brothers change the way people live today?
3. Are you like Wilbur and Orville Wright? Are you interested in new ideas? Do you like to build things? Explain.

LESSON 13: Introduction to Vowel Pairs, Vowel Digraphs, Diphthongs, and Phonograms   29

Your child is about to begin Unit 2 of Sadlier's *Word Study* program. In this unit, students will examine vowel pairs, vowel digraphs, diphthongs, and phonograms. The theme of this unit is the *Southeast,* including its people and history.

A **vowel pair** is two vowels sounded together to make one long vowel sound. The first vowel in the pair has the long sound of its name, and the second vowel is silent (br**ai**n, br**ee**ze).

A **vowel digraph** is two vowels sounded together to make a long or short sound (ch**ie**f, h**ea**d, sl**ei**gh), or a special sound (s**au**ce, str**aw,** b**oo**k).

A **diphthong** is two vowels blended together as one sound. Examples include p**oi**nt, j**oy**; sh**ou**t, fr**ow**n; st**ew.**

Family Focus

- Read together the passage on page 29. Discuss the impact of the Wright Brothers' achievement on modern life. Then reread the passage. Have your child identify words with vowel pairs, vowel digraphs, and diphthongs.

- Find Kitty Hawk, North Carolina, on a map. About how far is it from where you live? What route might your family take if you were to drive there? Make a plan together. List other places you might wish to see along the way.

LINKS TO LEARNING

To extend learning together, you might explore:

Web Sites
www.nps.gov/wrbr/
http://fly.to/AviationHistory

Videos
American Road Trips, Discovery Channel Video, 4 videos.

The Century: America's Time, Discovery Channel Video, 6 videos.

Literature
The Wright Brothers: How They Invented the Airplane by Russell Freedman, ©1991.

Outer Banks Mysteries and Seaside Stories by Charles Harry Whedbee, ©1980.

Name _____

Helpful Hint

A **vowel pair** is two vowels sounded together to make one long vowel sound. Here are eight vowel pairs:

ai   ay   ee   ei   ie   oa   oe   ow

The first vowel in the pair has the sound of its name, and the second vowel is silent. Listen:

Don't **delay** the **train.**   Can I **receive** a **free** pass?
Will you have some **pie?**   **Joe** has a **row boat.**

Say each word in the box below. Then sort the words by the sound that each vowel pair makes. Write each word in the correct column.

afraid   agree   approach   toe   deceive   doe   float   holiday   wait
mower   playful   free   seize   thirteen   spray   street   moan   rain

1 Long a	2 Long e	3 Long o

Underline the words in each sentence that have the *same* vowel sound as the sound given at the start of the row.

4. **Long** a   What an array of whole grains the market has!

5. **Long** i   She cried as she tried to peel the onion.

6. **Long** o   Joe bought a garden hoe and a bow tie.

CHALLENGE

Circle the vowel pairs in this word:

freeway

List other words with two vowel pairs.

Many **vowel pairs** build words with phonograms.
A **phonogram** is a syllable that has a vowel or vowels
plus one or more consonants. Phonograms have only
one vowel sound. Here are some phonograms:

ain	ay	oal	oat

**Use each phonogram and the letters given in the
boxes below to form words. Use the words to
complete the sentences.**

Foal

____oal

c	f	g	sh

1. This is a newborn horse. _____ 2. This is your aim or purpose. _____

3. Water is shallow here. _____ 4. Burn this mineral for heat. _____

____ain

pl	ch	tr	str

5. This means "not fancy." _____ 6. This is to stretch too far. _____

7. You make this with links. _____ 8. Another name for *railroad*. _____

Complete each sentence with a word from the box below.

decay	deceive	oath	praise	screeched	woe

9. The President takes a solemn _____ to defend the Constitution.

10. "_____ is me!" cried the doomed prisoner.

11. Teachers _____ students who put forth their best efforts.

12. Brush and floss your teeth regularly to prevent tooth _____.

13. The car _____ to a halt to avoid hitting the deer.

14. Did you _____ them by pretending to be asleep?

Home Involvement Activity Have your child underline
the vowel pairs in these words: **afloat** and **tiptoe.**
Together, list examples of words with the same vowel
pairs found on a page of your child's social studies book.

Name _____

Like a vowel pair, a **vowel digraph** is two vowels sounded together. Yet vowel digraphs do not follow the long vowel rule. A vowel digraph can make a **long** sound, a **short** sound, or a very **special** sound. Here are four vowel digraphs: ea ei ey ie.

h**ea**d   sl**ei**gh   ob**ey**   f**ie**ld   th**ie**f

When ea has the **long** e sound, as in n**ea**t or r**ea**ch, it is a **vowel pair.**

Street band playing in
New Orleans' French Quarter

Read aloud the words in bold type. Sort the words by the sound that each vowel digraph makes. Write each word in the correct column below.

three-**piece** band	bird of **prey**	good **neighbor**
steady beat	take a **survey**	**eight** days
strong **beliefs**	cotton **sweater**	amazing **wealth**
under **siege**	**instead** of milk	**grey** day
silver **shield**	**achieve** a goal	**leather** wallet

1 Short e	2 Long a	3 Long e
_____	_____	_____
_____	_____	_____
_____	_____	_____
_____	_____	_____
_____	_____	_____

> ## WORK TOGETHER

Get together with a partner. Write sentences that use words with the vowel digraphs ea, ei, ey, and ie. Sort the words according to short e, long a, or long e.

These **vowel digraphs** blend sounds together: au aw oo.

These two vowel digraphs stand for the **aw** sound. Listen:

Pau**l dr**aw**s.**

Now listen for two different sounds of oo:

The **c**oo**k sh**oo**k** the **sp**oo**n** to make it **c**oo**l.**

Write the vowel digraph au, aw, **or** oo **to complete each word.**

1	2	3	4
noteb____k	tr____p	h____k	dinos____r

5	6	7	8
h____d	s____ce	bl____m	jigs____puzzle

Complete each sentence with a word from the box below. Then circle the *spoon* **or the** *foot* **to show the** oo **sound in the word you wrote.**

baboon   barefoot   childhood   overlooks   seafood   teaspoon   good

9. The cabin _____ the Shenandoah Valley.

10. A trip to Savannah will give you a _____ history lesson.

11. One of my earliest _____ memories is of a trip to Florida.

12. The _____ is a kind of ape.

13. The recipe calls for one _____ of salt.

14. I love to walk _____ along a soft, sandy beach.

15. The North Carolina coast has great _____ restaurants.

LESSON 15: Vowel Digraphs
ea, ei, ey, ie, au, aw, oo

Home Involvement Activity Find words in a newspaper with the vowel digraphs ea, ei, ey, ie, au, aw, and oo. Listen for the sounds of the digraphs. Make a chart to sort the words by their vowel sounds.

Name _____

Read about a young girl's "dream" to be a country-music star.
Then answer the questions that follow.

In Music City, U.S.A.

Here I am in Nashville, Tennessee, the country music capital of the world. It's where the biggest country stars perform, and where I've always wanted to be.

Look at me, here on Music Row! Over here is the Country Music Hall of Fame. There is Ryman Auditorium. That's where the *Grand Ole Opry* used to be broadcast. My folks always listen to the live performances on the radio. They say that it's the nation's longest-running radio show. Nowadays, the show is broadcast from Music Valley on Opryland Drive. I'll just hop on the trolley that goes there. I hope it's not too late to get a ticket for today's show.

Well, I do get a ticket. It's right in the front row. I'm so excited! I've loved to sing ever since I was old enough to carry a tune. Some people say I'm pretty good, maybe even good enough to see my name in lights one day. No one stops me as I make my way up onto the stage and begin to wail. The star performer steps aside from the microphone and smiles.

The audience loves me. I can hardly believe it! I am making my singing debut at the *Grand Ole Opry!* Now the star is saying something. She's telling me…what? To wake up? Why is she…?

"Wake up, Ashley. It's late! The school bus will be here soon! Don't forget you have glee-club practice today."

"I know, Mom." Oh well, my adoring fans will just have to wait another night.

Reader's Response

1. **What clues let you know that the story is a dream?**

2. **Which parts of the story could be true? Which parts probably could not happen in real life?**

3. **Have you ever had a dream that you hoped would come true? Explain.**

READ & WRITE

Ashley dreams of becoming a country-music star. Do you have a dream like hers? How could you make your dream come true?

Think about a career that you would like to have someday. Write a story about how you might reach your goal. Be creative. Remember that in stories good things can happen! Use at least two of these words in your writing.

inspire dream follow goal believe speech achieve draw
career tried seize details disappointed road boast bloom

_____
_____
_____
_____
_____
_____
_____
_____
_____
_____
_____

Writer's Tip

Stories need a strong beginning, middle, and end. First, set the scene. Next, develop the characters and the action. Then, bring the story to a close.

Speaker's Challenge

Read your story aloud. Be an actor as you read. Think about how to get the tone of your story across to your listeners. For example, if the tone is humorous, read your story in a lighthearted way.

Name _____

> ### Helpful Hint
>
> A **diphthong** is two vowels that blend together to form one vowel sound.
> If you say a diphthong *very* slowly, you can hear both vowel sounds.
>
> The diphthongs **oi** in sp**oi**l and **oy** in b**oy** have the same vowel sound.
> The diphthong **ew** has the vowel sound you hear in ch**ew**.

Read each phrase below the three boxes. Underline the word in the phrase that has the diphthong oi, oy, or ew. Then write the word in the box below.

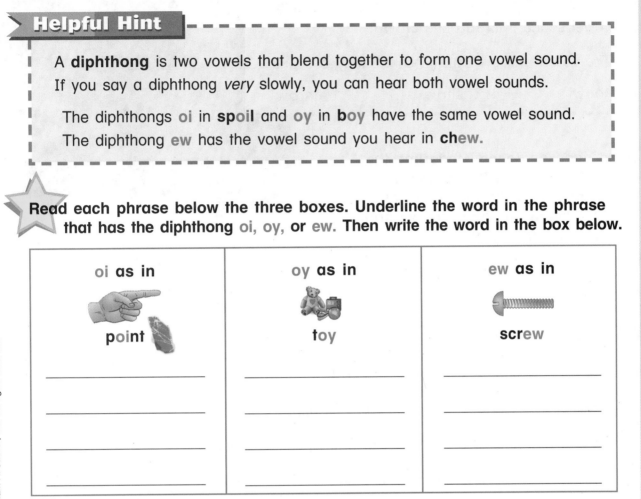

oi as in	oy as in	ew as in
point	toy	screw
_____	_____	_____
_____	_____	_____
_____	_____	_____
_____	_____	_____

1. sang a joyous song

2. outgrew her jacket

3. destroy the furniture

4. had a lovely singing voice

5. employ a programmer

6. had a shrewd idea

7. cancel your appointment

8. ate some oysters

9. renew the library books

10. join the photography club

11. ate some salty cashew nuts

12. wrapped in aluminum foil

> **CHALLENGE**
>
> Circle the diphthongs in these words:
>
> news
> trapezoid
> turquoise
>
> Which is a math word? A social studies word? An art word? List other words with diphthongs that you might use in math, science, gym, social studies, art, or music.

The **diphthongs** ou and ow can stand for the vowel sound in **cloud** and **clown**.

The **vowel pair** ow usually has the **long o** sound.

bowl   show   thr**ow**

Read each sentence. Underline the word that has the sound of ow. Then circle the *flower* 🍀 or the *bowl* 🥣 to show the ow sound in the underlined word.

The silversmith's shop in Colonial Williamsburg, Virginia

1. Williamsburg is a town with hundreds of tourists.

2. Let's browse through the silversmith's shop.

3. Look at that yellow hammer.

4. How far is Virginia Beach from here?

5. I can't sit near that rowdy group.

6. Has Williamsburg grown much in recent years?

7. Tomorrow we will tour the rest of the village.

8. Mom is allowing my brother to take us.

Complete each sentence with a word from the box below.

proud	houses	snow	brown	sounds	flows

9. She was _____ to be from Virginia.

10. Which body of water _____ through the state?

11. What charming _____ those birds make!

12. Does it ever _____ in Virginia?

13. The _____ look as they did long ago.

14. Many women's dresses are white and _____.

Home Involvement Activity Brainstorm ideas to create a list of words that have the diphthongs ou and ow, as in **mound** and **down**.

Name _____

Read each group of words. Say and spell each word in bold type. Repeat the word. Then sort the words according to their vowel sound. Write the words in the correct column below.

- **oath** of office

- **receives** a medal

- **overthrew** the dictator

- gave a rousing **speech**

- soothing **ointment**

- a happy **childhood**

- a heart filled with **woe**

- her first **choice**

- **praise** their efforts

- **loyalty** to the cause

- taking a **survey**

- may never **believe** me

- move with **caution**

- **grown** to respect them

- a helpful **neighbor**

- a **rowdy** group

- **threaten** to rain

- an imaginary **boundary**

Monticello, Thomas Jefferson's house in Virginia

Words with Vowel Pairs	Words with Vowel Digraphs	Words with Diphthongs

Some people call Virginia the "state of many Presidents." That's because Virginia leads all other states by far in the number of Presidents it has produced. To date, eight American Presidents have been born there.

Choose any President in American history. Write a brief biographical sketch of the person. Give key facts, such as place and date of birth, important family information, dates served as President, and achievements. Use three or more of these spelling words.

oath	receives	overthrew	speech	ointment	childhood
woe	choice	praise	loyalty	survey	believe
caution	grown	neighbor	rowdy	threaten	boundary

Name of President:

_____

_____

_____

_____

_____

_____

_____

_____

_____

_____

_____

Writer's Tip

A biographical sketch can't tell everything about a person's life. It is the writer's job to share with readers the most interesting or important details.

The White House in Washington, DC

Speaker's Challenge

With a partner, role-play a meeting between yourself and the President you wrote about. Let the biographical details come out in your "conversation."

Name _____

★ Read each group of words. Say the word in bold type and listen for its vowel sound. Cross out three words in the row that have a *different* vowel sound.

1	**receive** a gift	try	mean	play	believe	eye	deed
2	deep **voice**	vowel	joy	choice	vine	point	slice
3	**cloudy** day	brown	tough	cough	young	sound	round
4	**ready**, set, go	bed	steady	meal	head	vein	feed
5	**seize** the moment	praise	bread	yeast	key	blew	tease
6	**clown** around	crow	show	proud	doubt	rough	plow
7	birds of **prey**	vein	quaint	press	boat	grand	late
8	feelings of **grief**	siege	gripe	death	doe	team	leaf
9	**should** call	scout	stood	could	sauce	cool	wood
10	sore **throat**	flower	hoe	power	foot	grown	mow
11	**sprain** my wrist	arrow	friend	chase	spray	break	review
12	**browse** for food	grow	crown	four	though	loud	ground
13	great **wealth**	squeak	step	worth	spend	peach	feather
14	**zoom** lens	moon	comb	spoon	look	foot	smooth

★ Underline the word in each pair that has the *same* vowel sound as the sound given at the start of the row.

15. **Long a**   grain or grand?   tall or weigh?   toy or tray?

16. **Long e**   choice or cheese?   size or seize?   team or dread?

17. **Long i**   lie or leaf?   piece or pie?   receive or fly?

18. **Long o**   float or flute?   choose or coat?   woe or wool?

19. **Short e**   health or squeak?   deal or dead?   new or nest?

20. **Short u**   double or doubt?   would or young?   enough or shoulder?

Fill in the circle of the word that completes each sentence. Then write the word on the line.

1. Rich deposits of _____ lie beneath West Virginia.
   ○ coal   ○ breeze   ○ chain

2. Networks of _____ lines carry the ore from the mine areas.
   ○ praise   ○ train   ○ health

3. Mining does have its risks, but it can _____ many people.
   ○ review   ○ overlook   ○ employ

4. Miners _____ strict rules in order to be safe underground.
   ○ play   ○ show   ○ obey

Read each sentence. Choose the letter pair from the three in the row that completes both unfinished words. Write that same letter pair in both spaces.

5. Let's **foll**_____ that **fell**_____ to see which restaurant he picks.

6. Button your **c**_____**t** all the way to your **thr**_____**t**.

7. Emily has thoughts of garlic **br**_____**d** in her **h**_____**d**.

8. It took us **ab**_____**t** four days to paint the **h**_____**se**.

9. The **c**_____**k sh**_____**k** the wooden spoon.

10. Patricia **kn**_____ the people in the **n**_____**s**.

11. If you **del**_____ **spr**_____**ing** the rose bush, bugs may infest it.

12. The artist **redr**_____ the flowers that **gr**_____.

13. Ben will **dr**_____ a crab **cl**_____ to illustrate his sea garden.

14. The _____**ster** beds will be **destr**_____**ed** if we don't save the ocean.

aw	ew	ow
oi	oe	oa
ea	ei	ie
ow	ou	aw
oo	ou	ow
aw	ew	ow
ay	ai	ea
ea	ie	ew
aw	au	ee
oi	ou	oy

Extend & Apply

Write five sentences with two unfinished words that share the same vowel pairs, vowel digraphs, or diphthongs. Have a partner complete your words.

Name _____

Helpful Hint

You know that a **phonogram** is a syllable that has a vowel or vowels plus one or more consonants. Phonograms have only one vowel sound. Here are some phonograms:

all   ame   en   ight   ing   uck   ump

Notice how **phonograms** and **consonants** are combined in each of these words:

luck = l + **uck**   tightening = t + **ight** + **en** + **ing**

ballgame = b + **all** + g + **ame**

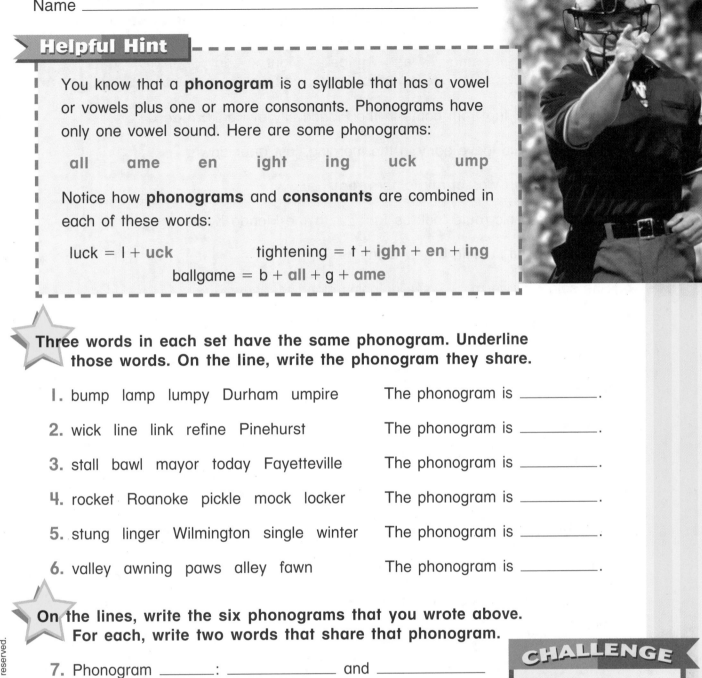

★ **Three words in each set have the same phonogram. Underline those words. On the line, write the phonogram they share.**

1. bump lamp lumpy Durham umpire   The phonogram is _____.

2. wick line link refine Pinehurst   The phonogram is _____.

3. stall bawl mayor today Fayetteville   The phonogram is _____.

4. rocket Roanoke pickle mock locker   The phonogram is _____.

5. stung linger Wilmington single winter   The phonogram is _____.

6. valley awning paws alley fawn   The phonogram is _____.

★ **On the lines, write the six phonograms that you wrote above. For each, write two words that share that phonogram.**

7. Phonogram _____ : _____ and _____

8. Phonogram _____ : _____ and _____

9. Phonogram _____ : _____ and _____

10. Phonogram _____ : _____ and _____

11. Phonogram _____ : _____ and _____

12. Phonogram _____ : _____ and _____

CHALLENGE

Nashville, Tennessee, and Asheville, North Carolina, are cities that have the phonogram **ash** in their names. Write the names of two Southern cities or towns that share a different phonogram.

⭐ **Add** the correct phonogram from the box to complete the word in each sentence. You'll need to use some phonograms more than once.

ale	all	ame	est	ide	ight	in	ink	ore

1. We begin our trip from home in the Florida city of Fort **Lauderd____**.

2. We **dec____** to leave early in the morning, just after dawn.

3. This early start was at my fathers **requ____**.

4. The long, scenic route took us far **____to** the Florida Keys.

5. My best friend Juanita **c____** along.

6. She said that we **m____** see dolphins along the way.

7. Our **d____ination** was the popular resort town of Key West.

8. Juanita had been there **bef____**. She spoke of its fabulous sunsets.

9. We arrived at our hotel at **nightf____**, just in time for dinner.

10. "We serve any fish you can **n____**," the waiter told us.

11. Juanita and I ordered the **yellowf____** tuna.

12. My parents were **del____ed** with the menu. They ordered pasta with fresh clams.

13. After dinner, we all walked barefoot along the beach in the **moonl____**.

14. On the following day, we explored the **t____pools** near our hotel.

15. I **th____** our wake-up call will be at 6:00 A.M. tomorrow. That's my dad for you!

LESSON 20: Combining Consonants with Phonograms

Home Involvement Activity Together, look at a map of Florida, the Sunshine State. Follow the route from Fort Lauderdale to Key West. Make a list of the places you spot along the way that contain the phonograms listed above.

Name _____

Helpful Hint

A **consonant blend** is two or three consonants sounded together so that each letter is heard. Notice how the **phonograms** and the **consonant blends** are combined in each of these words:

block = bl + **ock**   flight = fl + **ight**   scrap = scr + **ap**

★ **Complete the name of each picture. Combine the consonant blend in the box with one of the phonograms in the yellow box next to it.**

1	2
sn_____	fl_____
3	4
cl_____	cr_____

ane

ap

ock

ore

WORK TOGETHER

Get together with a partner to list as many words as you can that combine a consonant blend with the phonogram **ap** or **ight**. Then choose three words and write a sentence for each.

★ **Read about the writer Zora Neale Hurston. Fill in the circle of the word that completes each sentence. Then write the word on the line. Hint: Each answer combines a consonant blend with a phonogram.**

5. Zora was a _____ girl who grew up in the South.
   ○ bright   ○ thin   ○ tired

6. She loved to listen to stories told in the general _____.
   ○ store   ○ ship   ○ pharmacy

7. Later, she studied anthropology and took _____ through the South.
   ○ caps   ○ trips   ○ chores

8. She used her experiences to write about _____-town life.
   ○ poor   ○ small   ○ shop

Zora Neale Hurston
(1903–1960)

⭐ **Each box gives three consonant blends and three phonograms. Match the blends and the phonograms in each box to build three words. Then write the words on the lines.**

1			2			3		
cl		ide	gr		orts	pr		aces
st		imb	sp		eat	fl		ices
pr		ate	spr		ings	pl		at

_____   _____   _____

_____   _____   _____

_____   _____   _____

⭐ **Use a word from the boxes above to complete each sentence about West Virginia, the Mountain State.**

4. With a population of about 2 million, West Virginia is

   the 35th largest _____.

5. About two-thirds of the state is _____.

6. Yet there are also hills and mountains to _____.

7. West Virginia boasts _____ that tourists can afford.

8. It also offers interesting _____ to see.

9. For example, you might take a dip in one of

   the state's mineral water _____.

10. Harpers Ferry is another _____ place to visit.

11. Skiers can enjoy winter _____ at the Snowshoe Ski Resort.

12. The state parks are another source of

    state _____.

Harpers Ferry, West Virginia

 Home Involvement Activity Imagine that relatives or family friends are visiting your state for the first time. List some top tourist attractions in your area. Which do you like best? Which might they like? Talk about why.

Name _____

Helpful Hints

Many words combine **consonant blends** and **phonograms.** Look at these examples:

flake = fl + **ake**   prank = pr + **ank**

Some words can have more than one **consonant blend** and one **phonogram.**

screenplay = scr + **een** + pl + **ay**

Sprockets

Each pair of words has the same phonogram. Find the phonogram and underline it in both words.

1. sprocket   smock   2. spice   splice   3. blink   crinkle

4. bright   frightful   5. plump   trumpet   6. request   presto

7. strainer   drainage   8. crankshaft blanket   9. explore   restore

10. strip   clipper   11. hideaway   bride   12. squall   mall

Write a word from above to complete each statement.

13. To travel in an unknown place is to _____.

14. Something that causes fear is _____.

15. An Italian word meaning "fast" is _____.

16. To separate liquids from solids, you could use

    a _____.

17. To cause to wrinkle is to _____.

18. A covering for a bed is a _____.

19. An apronlike garment worn over clothing is

    a _____.

20. A musical instrument is a _____.

WORD STRATEGY

Words with two or more syllables can have more than one consonant blend and one phonogram. To unlock a long word, look for blends and phonograms. Try it:

   blacksnake
   bridegroom

Write a sentence for each word.

Read the twelve words in the box. Four phonograms appear three times each. Write these four phonograms on the lines below.

> | | | | | |
> |---|---|---|---|---|
> | clay | smoke | sprinkler | clipping | drink | crayfish |
> | brink | slipshod | broke | stray | spoke | trip |

1. _____ 2. _____ 3. _____ 4. _____

Use the words from the box above to complete the sentences.

5. It's a good idea to _____ plenty of water in the hot sun.

6. Another word for *voyage* is _____.

7. I cut out the newspaper _____ that had a photograph of my dog.

8. Mom let me keep the _____ cat I found.

9. Roberto made puppets out of modeling _____.

10. I was on the _____ of tears when I didn't make the team.

11. The plumbers did a _____ job, and the pipe burst.

12. Three synonyms of _____ are *cracked, fractured,* and *split.*

13. _____ look like little lobsters.

14. The past tense of *speak* is _____.

15. Dad installed a new _____ system for watering our lawn.

16. Thick black _____ covered the Everglades as the fire raged.

LESSON 22: Combining More
Consonant Blends with Phonograms

Home Involvement Activity Look over the words from this lesson. Try to make up a funny story that uses several of the words. Take turns telling your stories. Tape-record the best ones to play back and assess at a later time.

⭐ **Read about how people are rescuing the Everglades from pollution. Then answer the questions that follow.**

Saving the Everglades

from a nonfiction article in Time for Kids magazine

FLORIDA

Everglades

Everglades National Park in Florida doesn't look like much from an airplane. But a closer look shows a busy natural world. Hundreds of kinds of animals live in the Everglades.

But the Everglades is in serious trouble. After years of bad planning, the Everglades is dying. Dozens of its many animals are threatened. Some of its plants and flowers are disappearing. But help for the Everglades is under way. Humans are rescuing the Everglades and its wildlife from death by pollution.

When large numbers of people first moved to Florida more than a century ago, the Everglades was thought to be nothing but swampland. Builders tried to drain the swamp. Farms and cities sprang up where alligators used to run freely. In the 1920s, engineers straightened rivers. They hoped to stop flooding and keep water supplies stable for farms and cities. The plan worked.

But the changes also harmed the Everglades. The area shrank in size by half. Much of the fresh water disappeared. And the numbers of birds, alligators, and other animals shrank, too.

Now everyone is aware of the importance of the Everglades. Farmers are aware of the dangers of the chemicals they are using. And engineers are putting rivers back on their old winding courses. In all, billions of dollars will be spent to help the Everglades. For most people, that is money well spent.

📖 Reader's Response

1. **What happened to Florida's Everglades?**

2. **How are people trying to save the Everglades today?**

3. **Compare the Everglades with another place that has been hurt by pollution. How are the two places alike? What are the differences?**

You probably know that alligators and crocodiles are cousins. But did you know that the Everglades is the only place in the United States where American alligators and crocodiles live together? Look at the pictures below. Can you tell the difference between an alligator and a crocodile? How?

⭐ **Write one or more paragraphs that compare the American alligator with the American crocodile. Do some research. Describe at least two ways that these animals are alike. Then write about their differences. Include a drawing. Use at least two of these words.**

American alligator

Words to Show Similarities:	both	similarly	in the same way
	like	alike	by comparison
Words to Show Differences:	but	yet	however	unlike
	by contrast		differs from

_____

_____

_____

_____

_____

_____

_____

_____

_____

Writer's Tip

Make a comparison chart before writing. In one column, list how the animals are alike. In the other column, list how they are different. Use your chart to write your essay.

Writer's Challenge

Choose two animals that are similar, such as a panda and a raccoon or a panda and a bear. In a paragraph, explain how these two animals are alike. Then describe their differences. Compare the two animals' size and shape as well as their diet and habits. Summarize your "findings" at the end.

American crocodile

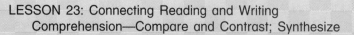

Name _____

Complete the name of each picture by combining the consonant digraph in the box with one of the phonograms in the yellow box below.

| ack | alk | orn | ip |

1	2	3	4
th_____	wh_____	ch_____	sh_____

Read about South Carolina's Spoleto Festival. Write the word from the yellow box below that completes each sentence. Note that each word combines a consonant digraph with a phonogram.

| things | chance | where | shares |

5. South Carolina is _____ the Spoleto Festival takes place every year.

6. The state's largest port, Charleston, _____ this arts festival with the world.

7. Visitors can watch dancers dance, hear singers sing, and do many other interesting _____.

8. Although the festival attracts famous artists, it also gives local performers the _____ to perform.

WORK TOGETHER

Work with a group. List music-related words, such as song titles or instruments, that combine a consonant digraph with a phonogram.

⭐ **Add the correct phonogram from the box to complete the word in each sentence. Use a phonogram only once.**

ame	are	at	est	ill	ine	ing	ink	ock	uck

1. Is there another town with the same name as your town? Which one

   took the name first is probably the furth_____ thing from your mind.

2. You might th_____ that people don't care about such things.

3. However, the people of Wash_____ton, Georgia, care very much.
   This town claims to be the first town named for our very first President.

4. This claim might get a ch_____y reception in other towns with that name.

5. The people of Washington, North Carolina, for one,

   would be sh_____ed to hear of Georgia's claim.

6. In Washington, North Carolina, people say th_____ the
   honor of being the first town named for George Washington
   belongs to them.

7. These people would ch_____le at Georgia's claim. They
   would politely explain that Washington actually visited their
   town in 1791.

8. One town that used to sh_____ in this "competition"
   was Washington, Kentucky, but this is no longer the case.

9. In 1990, this town left the battle with barely a wh_____ or
   a whimper. In that year, the town joined with a neighboring
   town and took the name "Old Washington."

10. Yet the battle still rages in other towns, and the claim

    for Washington's n_____ lives on.

A statue of George Washington

⭐ **Choose two of the words you wrote above. On the lines below, write a sentence for each of the words.**

11. _____

12. _____

Home Involvement Activity Many towns and cities share the same name, like Springfield or Portland. With your family, brainstorm a list of places with identical names. How many can you list?

Name _____

Combine the phonogram in each box and the consonants, consonant blends, and consonant digraphs to form words below.

1 **ain**	2 **ake**	3 **op**
r_____y	f_____	sl_____py
gr_____	br_____	st_____ped
ch_____	clamb_____	dr_____ping
dr_____pipe	milksh_____	l_____sided
eyestr_____	sn_____root	sharecr_____per

Use each phonogram below and the consonants, consonant blends, and consonant digraphs in the yellow boxes to form words. Then use the words to complete the sentences.

_____aw | s   cl   th   str |

4. Drink your milkshake with a _____.

5. Some animals can grow a new _____.

6. The past tense of *see* is _____.

7. You'll need to _____ the steak before eating it.

_____oke | y   str   br |

8. The team of oxen are in a _____.

9. The rope _____ under the weight.

10. The golfer led by one _____ after the first round.

A **hink-pink** is a pair of 1-syllable words that rhyme.   **square chair**

A **hinky-pinky** is a pair of 2-syllable words that rhyme.   **quicker ticker**

A **hinkity-pinkity** is a pair of 3-syllable words that rhyme.   **persistent assistant**

These word pairs combine consonants with phonograms.

All three of these rhyming word pairs also have meaning.

Note that **reachable teachable** is not a hinkity-pinkity.

It rhymes, but it has no real meaning on its own.

Complete each sentence by writing the other half of the hink-pink, hinky-pinky, or hinkity-pinkity. Choose words from the box below. Be careful! Just because the words rhyme doesn't mean that they are spelled alike.

latitude	woolly	drab	French	frock	hefty
election	shocking	standing	couch	fleeting	construction

1. When we saw the strange clothing in the fashion show, we went into

   _____ **shock.**

2. A person who sits on the sofa and complains is a _____ **grouch.**

3. The gymnast made a _____ **landing** after her vault.

4. In a Paris park, we sat down on a _____ **bench.**

5. The overweight left-handed pitcher is quite a _____ **lefty.**

6. Our quick get-together was a _____ **meeting.**

7. My friend in the candidate's office is my _____ **connection.**

8. A boring conversation is filled with _____ **blab.**

9. If you insist that your town is located in the very best position, you

   have a _____ **attitude.**

10. Anything that slows down building is a _____ **obstruction.**

11. An unexpected loud banging on your door is a _____ **knocking.**

12. That big, mean, nasty sheep is a _____ **bully.**

 Home Involvement Activity Make up your own hink-pinks, hinky-pinkies, and hinkity-pinkities. Say them aloud to each other for some **winning grinning!**

Name _____

⭐ **Read about how a new discovery in Virginia is showing people what life was like in Jamestown, the first permanent English settlement in North America. Then answer the questions that follow.**

Digging Up the Past

from a nonfiction article in Time for Kids magazine

Brent Smith of Houston, Texas, cannot take his eyes off the skeleton. Lying in a glass case at the National Geographic Society in Washington, D.C., the skeleton is a mystery. "I just need to know what happened to this guy," says Brent. "What was his name? How did he die?"

James Fort Construction, May–June 1607

That's what historians are wondering, too. The skeleton is nearly 400 years old. It was found in Jamestown, Virginia, site of the first permanent English settlement in America. For years, people thought that the old fort there had been washed away by the James River. But new discoveries, including this skeleton, prove that the fort and its clues to colonial life are buried under the soil.

On May 13, 1607, a ship carrying 104 men and boys from England arrived in Virginia. They named their settlement Jamestown, after Britain's King James. The colonists built a triangle-shaped fort along the river to protect themselves.

Eventually, Jamestown, Virginia's capital, was moved to nearby Williamsburg. Jamestown began to disappear—at least above ground. But what about underground? In April 1994, archaeologist Bill Kelso and others found bits of pottery that could only have been from the 1607 fort. "That first day, we knew we had found it!"

The discoveries are giving scientists and historians the best picture ever of how early colonists lived. They hope to come up with more answers for kids like Brent Smith.

📖 Reader's Response

1. **What is happening today in Jamestown, Virginia? Why is it important?**

2. **What is the main idea of this article?**

3. **If you could speak to one of the Jamestown settlers, what would you say? Why?**

Scientists have uncovered skeletons, armor, beads, keys, pottery, and toys from the original Jamestown settlement. So far, more than 180,000 items have been uncovered, and the digging is still going on! All these discoveries are showing people how the original colonists lived 400 years ago.

Make a list of items that you and your classmates could put in a time capsule for scientists to find 400 years from now. Your list might include maps, sports equipment, and computers. Then write a paragraph explaining what these items would tell about you and the twenty-first century. State a clear main idea and give your details in logical order. Summarize your ideas at the end. Use at least two of these words.

explain	demonstrate	discover	scientists	historians
to begin with	besides	also	however	now
then	on the other hand		as a result	finally

_____

_____

_____

_____

_____

_____

_____

_____

Writer's Tip

Use **transition words,** such as *to begin with, however,* and *finally,* to show how your ideas are related. Some transition words can also help you combine shorter sentences.

Speaker's Challenge

Use the paragraph you wrote to give a speech about what people might find if they "uncovered" your time capsule in the future. Make an outline of your main idea and details. Include a good topic sentence at the beginning and a strong summary at the end.

Name _____

Circle the letter of the word in each row that has the same vowel sound as the phonogram in red.

1. grain   **a.** grind   **b.** grin   **c.** crane

2. broke   **a.** croak   **b.** streak   **c.** break

3. pale   **a.** reality   **b.** sail   **c.** steeple

4. paw   **a.** claw   **b.** cow   **c.** blow

5. cake   **a.** eke   **b.** weak   **c.** steak

6. play   **a.** rely   **b.** maintain   **c.** ready

7. blink   **a.** blank   **b.** arch   **c.** crinkle

8. shame   **a.** claim   **b.** steam   **c.** sham

9. flight   **a.** caught   **b.** kite   **c.** ought

10. slide   **a.** rawhide   **b.** lid   **c.** bleed

Read each sentence. Choose the phonogram from the three in the row that completes _both_ unfinished words. Write that phonogram in both spaces.

op	ip	up
ink	ing	ick
oke	ash	ight
aw	an	at
unk	eat	ill
ock	oke	ick
ale	ance	ice
on	ug	in
ash	or	ay
all	ine	ump

11. They **ch____ped** off the last act of the very long ____**era**.

12. I **th____** I know why the stars **tw____le** in the sky.

13. To my **del____**, we danced until **midn____**.

14. Our teacher **overs____** the care of a rare tropical **mac____**.

15. The **bl____ing** sheep totally **def____ed** my chance to sleep.

16. It was **sh____ing** when the manager **padl____ed** the door.

17. If you want my **adv____**, it's not worth the **sacrif____**.

18. Dad bought an ____**ly** new **pl____** for the toaster.

19. Firefighters **spr____ed** water on the **runw____**.

20. How well can you **rec____** the plays in **baseb____**?

Read this passage about Florida's Everglades. For each numbered blank, there is a choice of words below. Circle the letter of the word that best completes the sentence.

The Florida Everglades is a large region of flat, low land. Much of the year, slowly **1** water covers it. In places, the Everglades has **2** of tall, sharp <u>saw grass</u>. There are also small tree islands called hammocks. Deer, panthers, and **3** live on the hammocks.

You have read that in the past, people **4** parts of the Everglades. They dug canals and built roads there for Florida's growing population. Yet development had a high cost. It caused fires and threatened to endanger the land's natural water cycles and animals. People soon saw that if the **5** disappeared, so would the fresh water supply for Florida's cities.

Florida needs the Everglades. It must save its plants and animals. It must protect its water supply. These are great challenges. Luckily, Florida has been taking steps in the **6** direction. The Everglades is now a national park, protected by government laws.

1. **a.** flowing **b.** floating **c.** flapping   2. **a.** foods **b.** choices **c.** fields

3. **a.** beaks **b.** bears **c.** breaks   4. **a.** drained **b.** chained **c.** grained

5. **a.** highlands **b.** headlands **c.** wetlands   6. **a.** mighty **b.** nightly **c.** right

Read the passage again to answer these questions. Circle the letter of the correct answer.

7. The author feels that the Everglades should be
   a. drained and covered.
   b. painted and photographed.
   c. protected and preserved.
   d. developed and burned.

8. The word <u>saw grass</u> probably got its name from its
   a. short, thick, grasses.
   b. sea islands.
   c. wispy stems.
   d. tall, sharp, teethlike leaves.

Airboat exploring the Everglades

Extend & Apply

In a sentence, state the problem faced by Florida's Everglades. In a second sentence, suggest a way to solve it.

The Heart of the Country

The Middle West has been called the breadbasket of the United States. There, in the heart of the country, this land produces wheat and corn for the nation. Yet in 1871, fire raged through the largest city in America's heartland. After two days of fire, Chicago lay in ruins.

The great Chicago fire of 1871 killed 300 people, left 90,000 homeless, and destroyed 18,000 buildings. It ruined businesses, too. Yet it couldn't destroy Chicago's location on Lake Michigan. From its important placement in the Midwest, Chicago linked the industrial cities of the Northeast with the farms and ranches of the West. As soon as the rubble was cleared, Chicago began to build a new city from the ground up.

Luckily, architects and city planners had two important new tools. They could work with a strong new material—steel. They could also use a new invention—the elevator. With these two improvements, architects could build high into the sky. One new skyscraper after another was built. Chicago soon had an impressive skyline.

Today, you can see the results of this remarkable construction. Yet there is more to see in Chicago than just tall buildings. Chicago is as beautiful on the ground as it is high above.

💡 Critical Thinking

1. **What caused the people of Chicago to rebuild the city?**

2. **What effect did this rebuilding have on Chicago?**

3. **Do you think you would like to be an architect someday? Give reasons for your answer.**

Dear Family,

In Unit 3, your child will explore and use word endings, contractions, plurals, possessives, and compound words. The theme of this unit is the *Middle West*, including its people and history.

A **contraction** usually combines two words into one by leaving out one or more letters. An **apostrophe** (') shows where the missing letter or letters were. Examples of contractions are **I'm** (*I am*), **doesn't** (*does not*), and **aren't** (*are not*).

A **possessive noun** shows ownership. An **apostrophe** and an **s** (**'s**) are used to form a singular possessive noun (one **mayor's** plan) or a plural possessive noun not ending in **s** (the **men's** ties). An apostrophe alone is used to form most plural possessives (two **girls'** books).

A **compound** word is made up of two or more smaller words. Your child often uses compound words, such as **backpack** and **homework.**

Sidebar article

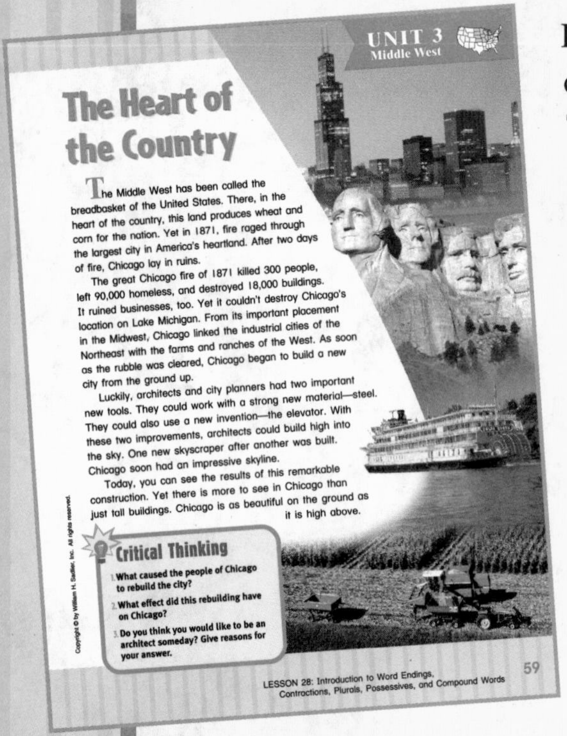

UNIT 3
Middle West

The Heart of the Country

The Middle West has been called the breadbasket of the United States. There, in the heart of the country, this land produces wheat and corn for the nation. Yet in 1871, fire raged through the largest city in America's heartland. After two days of fire, Chicago lay in ruins.

The great Chicago fire of 1871 killed 300 people, left 90,000 homeless, and destroyed 18,000 buildings. It ruined businesses, too. Yet it couldn't destroy Chicago's location on Lake Michigan. From its important placement in the Midwest, Chicago linked the industrial cities of the Northeast with the farms and ranches of the West. As soon as the rubble was cleared, Chicago began to build a new city from the ground up.

Luckily, architects and city planners had two important new tools. They could work with a strong new material—steel. They could also use a new invention—the elevator. With these two improvements, architects could build high into the sky. One new skyscraper after another was built. Chicago soon had an impressive skyline.

Today, you can see the results of this remarkable construction. Yet there is more to see in Chicago than just tall buildings. Chicago is as beautiful on the ground as it is high above.

Critical Thinking

1. What caused the people of Chicago to rebuild the city?
2. What effect did this rebuilding have on Chicago?
3. Do you think you would like to be an architect someday? Give reasons for your answer.

LESSON 28: Introduction to Word Endings, Contractions, Plurals, Possessives, and Compound Words   59

Family Focus

- Together, look at a map of the United States. Identify the states of the Middle West: Illinois, Indiana, Iowa, Kansas, Michigan, Minnesota, Missouri, Nebraska, Ohio, North Dakota, South Dakota, and Wisconsin. Talk about the states you would like to visit.

- The Middle West hosts many professional sports teams. Work together to list baseball, basketball, football, soccer, and hockey teams whose fields or stadiums are in this region.

LINKS TO LEARNING

To extend learning together, you might explore:

Web Sites
www.ci.chi.il.us

www.chicagohistory.net/history/fire.html

Video
The Mighty Mississippi, Discovery Channel Video, 2 videos.

Literature
Chicago by R. Conrad Stein, ©1997.

A Place Called Freedom by Scott Russell Sanders, ©1997.

Name _____

Helpful Hints

Add **s**, **ed**, or **ing** to most **base words** to make a new word.

talk**s**   talk**ed**   talk**ing**

Add **es** to words that end in **s**, **ss**, **ch**, **sh**, **x**, **z**, or **zz**.

guess**es**   teach**es**   crush**es**   box**es**   fizz**es**

When a **base word** ends in a **consonant** followed by **y**, change the **y** to **i** before adding **es** or **ed**. Just add **ing** to words that end in **y**.

scurr**y** → scurr**ies**   scurr**ied**   scurry**ing**

⭐ Add **s** or **es**, **ed**, and **ing** to each base word. Change **y** to **i** as needed. Write the new words on the lines.

Base Word	Add s or es	Add ed	Add ing
1. marry	_____	_____	_____
2. reach	_____	_____	_____
3. relax	_____	_____	_____
4. impress	_____	_____	_____
5. rush	_____	_____	_____
6. bully	_____	_____	_____
7. buzz	_____	_____	_____
8. select	_____	_____	_____

⭐ **Write the base word for each word below.**

9. mixing _____   10. kisses _____

11. geniuses _____   12. carrying _____

13. waltzed _____   14. sketches _____

15. rallied _____   16. frizzes _____

CHALLENGE

Use the spelling strategies you have just learned to add **s** or **es**, **ed**, and **ing** to the words below. Then write a sentence for one form of each word.

    fix
    screech
    crash
    hurry

When a **base word** ends in **silent** e, drop the **final** e before adding **ed** or **ing.** For most words ending in **silent** e, keep the e when adding **s.**

bak**e** → bak**ed** bak**ing** bak**es**   eras**e** → eras**ed** eras**ing** eras**es**

When a **base word** with one syllable ends in one **vowel** followed by a **consonant,** usually double the final consonant before adding **ed** or **ing.**

p**at** + **ed** = pa**tted**   br**ag** + **ing** = bra**gging**   sh**ip** + **ing** = shi**pping**

For most two-syllable words ending in one **vowel** and one **consonant,** double the consonant only if the accent is on the second syllable.

perm**it** + **ed** = permi**tted**   occ**ur** + **ing** = occu**rring**

★ **The following sentences tell about an unusual project that honors a brave Native American. Add s or es, ed, or ing to each base word in parentheses (). Write the new words on the lines.**

1. A sculptor _____ many unusual techniques. (apply)

2. One creative man _____ half his life to turning a mountain in South Dakota into a work of art. (commit)

3. Polish-American Korczak Ziolkowski proposed _____ a huge monument to honor Crazy Horse, the great chief of the Oglala Sioux nation. (create)

Crazy Horse Memorial still under construction

4. He was just _____ when he predicted it would take him 30 years. (guess)

5. Korczak knew that such a huge project would require a lot of _____. (plan)

6. _____ in 1958, he set off the first blast on Thunderhead Mountain in the Black Hills. (Begin)

7. He worked on that mountain for years, _____ stone into a magnificent sculpture. (shape)

8. After _____ nearly 36 years to the Crazy Horse project, time ran out for the artist. (give)

9. Korczak died, _____ an incomplete statue and unfinished dreams. (leave)

Home Involvement Activity Beat, burst, and **cut** are verbs that are the same in the present and in the past tense. Work together to make a list of other verbs that do not change from the present to the past.

Name _____

Helpful Hint

A **contraction** usually combines two words into one by leaving out one or more letters. An **apostrophe** (') shows where the missing letter or letters were.

it + is = **it's**   is + not = **isn't**   do + not = **don't**   will + not = **won't**

I + have = **I've**   you + are = **you're**   he + would = **he'd**   we + will = **we'll**

Write the contraction for each pair of words. Then write the letter or letters that have been left out of the contraction.

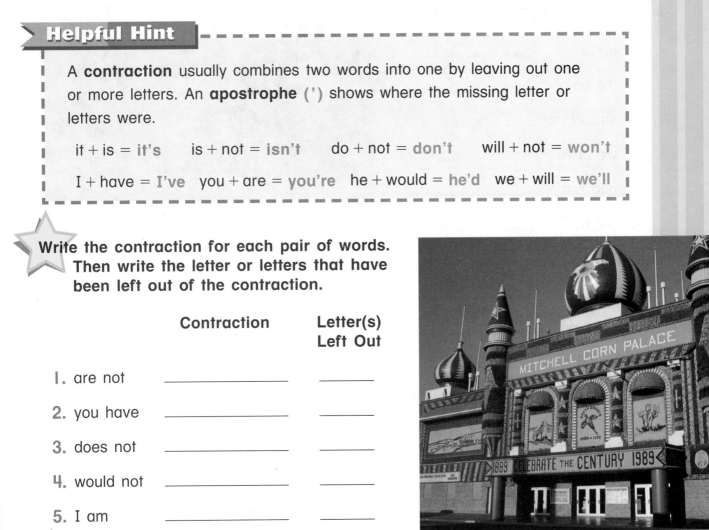

	Contraction	Letter(s) Left Out
1. are not	_____	_____
2. you have	_____	_____
3. does not	_____	_____
4. would not	_____	_____
5. I am	_____	_____

The sentences below are about the amazing Corn Palace in Mitchell, South Dakota. Underline the contraction in each sentence. Then write the two words for which each contraction stands.

6. In Mitchell, South Dakota, they're just nuts about corn.

   _____ _____

7. Mitchell is where you'll see the famous Corn Palace.

   _____ _____

8. What's most striking about the Corn Palace is that its outside is covered with South Dakota corn and grain!

   _____ _____

WORK TOGETHER

With a group, list the features of a special building in your town. Then write two short passages that describe the building. Use contractions in one description but none in the other. Compare the passages. Which do you prefer? Why?

⭐ **Read the words. Write their contractions on the lines.**

1. he is _____

2. did not _____

3. should not _____

4. we have _____

5. had not _____

6. will not _____

7. he will _____   12. could not _____

8. Bob is _____   13. he has _____

9. does not _____   14. they have _____

10. would not _____   15. she is _____

11. she would _____   16. I will _____

Scene from the movie *It's a Wonderful Life*, 1946

⭐ **These movie, book, and song titles should have contractions. Rewrite each title correctly by using a contraction.**

17. *It Is a Wonderful Life* _____

18. "Let Us Fall in Love" _____

19. "Who Is That Knocking?" _____

20. *You Have Got Mail* _____

21. "Do Not Be Cruel" _____

22. *We Are No Angels* _____

23. *Look Who Is Talking* _____

24. *You Cannot Go Home Again* _____

25. "You Are My Everything" _____

26. *I Have Heard the Mermaids Singing* _____

Home Involvement Activity Brainstorm another list of movie, book, or song titles that have contractions. Work together to replace each contraction with the words for which it stands.

Name _____

Helpful Hints

Plural means "more than one." Add **s** to make most **base words** plural.

farm + **s** = farm**s**   rope + **s** = rope**s**   statue + **s** = statue**s**

Add **es** to words that end in **s, ss, ch, sh, x, z,** or **zz**.

geniu**s** + **es** = geniu**ses**   di**sh** + **es** = di**shes**   walt**z** + **es** = walt**zes**

⭐ **Add s or es to form the plural of each word.
Write the plural word on the line.**

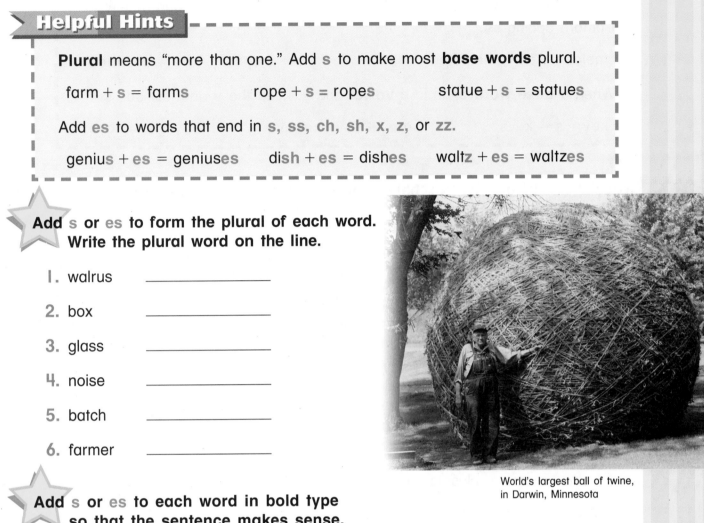

1. walrus _____

2. box _____

3. glass _____

4. noise _____

5. batch _____

6. farmer _____

World's largest ball of twine,
in Darwin, Minnesota

⭐ **Add s or es to each word in bold type
so that the sentence makes sense.
Write the new plural word on the line.**

7. One of our **wish** was to see the world's _____
largest ball of twine.

8. In fact, two Midwestern towns boast
very large **ball** of twine. The one in Darwin,
Minnesota, measures 12 feet across! _____

9. A man from Cawker City, Kansas, liked
challenge, so he made his own ball of twine.
But his had a diameter of only 11 feet. _____

10. These two creations were made without
paint, **brush,** or other art supplies. Both
are on display in their Midwestern towns. _____

CHALLENGE

Brainstorm ideas
to create a list of
movies, television
programs, songs,
books, stories, or
poems that have
plural words in their
titles. Circle each
plural word on
your list.

When a **base word** ends in a **consonant** followed by **y**, change the **y** to **i** before adding **es.**

melo**dy** + **es** = melo**dies**   coun**ty** + **es** = coun**ties**

When a **base word** ends in a **vowel** and **y**, keep the **y** and just add **s.**

ke**y** + **s** = ke**ys**   journe**y** + **s** = journe**ys**   bo**y** + **s** = bo**ys**

Use a word from the box below for each clue in the puzzle. Write one letter in each space. Then read down the shaded column to answer the question at the bottom.

stories	pantries	poppies	delays	buoys
paddies	currencies	injuries	dairies	bodies

1. money used in different countries
   — — — — — — — — —

2. floating objects used to warn ships
   — — — — —

3. our physical shapes
   — — — — — —

4. small rooms or closets for storing food
   — — — — — — — —

5. series of wrongs done to someone
   — — — — — — — —

6. postponements
   — — — — — —

7. round, showy red flowers
   — — — — — — —

8. farms where milk cows are raised
   — — — — — — —

9. fields where rice is grown
   — — — — — — —

10. tales of fictional or true events
    — — — — — — —

Question: Which town in Iowa is building the world's largest ear of corn— a 50-foot giant?

Answer: _____

Home Involvement Activity The following farm-related words are scrambled. They are also in the plural form. Unscramble the words and write a sentence for each one.
lossi   lebasst   sdraynrab   seidlf   ratcrost

Name _____

For most words ending in **f**, **lf**, or **fe**, form the plural by changing the **f** to **v** and adding **es**.

loa**f** = loa**ves**   wo**lf** = wo**lves**   kni**fe** = kni**ves**

There are some exceptions to this rule. You form the plural of some words ending in **f**, **lf**, or **fe** and most words ending in **ff** by adding **s**.

gu**lf** = gulf**s**   sa**fe** = safe**s**   cli**ff** = cliff**s**

Write the plural form of each word.

1. leaf _____   2. calf _____

3. half _____   4. life _____

5. belief _____   6. bluff _____

7. reef _____   8. shelf _____

Complete each sentence with the plural form of a word from the box. Look in a dictionary if you need help.

| sniff | thief | roof | safe | loaf | wharf |

9. Violent tornadoes in the Midwest had destroyed the

town and both _____, or docks.

A Midwestern tornado

10. All the houses in the village once had red _____.

11. We hoped that the new alarm system would prevent

_____ from looting the stores.

12. New _____ were installed in the bank to protect the money of the merchants and townspeople.

13. After several _____, the police dog decided that there were no survivors in the rubble.

14. _____ of bread were given to the victims.

CHALLENGE

Each of these words has two plural forms. Write the two plurals. Then write a sentence for one of the plural forms of each word.

hoof

scarf

staff

For most words ending in o after a **vowel,** add s to form the plural.

studio + s = studios   igloo + s = igloos

For most words ending in o after a **consonant,** add es to form the plural.

tomato + es = tomatoes   hero + s = heroes

However, there are many exceptions. For some words that end in o, just add s.

piano = pianos   auto = autos

Write the plural form of each word. If you aren't sure whether to add s or es, look in a dictionary.

1. video _____   2. torpedo _____

3. radio _____   4. photo _____

5. potato _____   6. oboe _____

7. duo _____   8. rodeo _____

9. banjo _____   10. lasso _____

Write the plural form of the eight words below. Then circle those eight plural words in the puzzle. The words can appear across, on a slant, or up and down.

11. echo _____

12. cello _____

13. half _____

14. solo _____

15. poncho _____

16. soprano _____

17. oaf _____

18. self _____

s	e	o	r	a	i	d	s	s
o	c	a	u	f	f	s	o	e
p	h	f	c	h	o	l	l	l
r	o	s	c	e	o	t	o	v
a	e	s	r	c	l	a	s	e
n	s	e	g	e	l	l	o	s
o	t	i	p	r	u	x	o	e
s	p	h	a	l	v	e	s	s
d	p	o	n	c	h	o	s	e

Workers assembling **auto**s at a Michigan auto plant

Home Involvement Activity Work together to look through some newspapers or magazines. Circle the plural form of words ending in f, lf, fe, ff, and o.

Name _____

Helpful Hints

The **plurals** of some words do not have **s** or **es** at the end.
These words become plural in irregular ways.

man → **men**   foot → **feet**   tooth → **teeth**   goose → **geese**

Some words stay the same whether singular or plural.

gross   series   species   trout   deer   sheep   moose

★ **Read the irregular plural forms in the box below. Write each plural on the line next to the singular form of the word.**

children   lice   crises   oases   mice   oxen
teeth   feet   media   parentheses   men   women

1. mouse _____   2. child _____   3. woman _____

4. ox _____   5. louse _____   6. crisis _____

7. foot _____   8. tooth _____   9. man _____

10. oasis _____   11. medium _____   12. parenthesis _____

★ **All the words below have the same singular and plural form. Write each word under the correct category. The first answer is given.**

alfalfa   bacon   asparagus   wheat   cattle
cod   deer   bison   spinach   popcorn

Plant Kingdom	Animal Kingdom
alfalfa	bacon

WORD STRATEGY

The saying "Rules are made to be broken" is true for some plurals. Check a dictionary to write the *two* plural forms for these words:

fungus   index
radius   appendix

Every clue for this crossword puzzle is given in singular form. To solve the puzzle, write the plural form for each of the clues.

Across

1. safe
3. rope
5. man
7. index
9. alfalfa
12. shelf
13. noise
15. series
18. deer
20. eight
24. species
25. moose
26. oasis

Down

2. fungus
3. radius
4. parenthesis
5. medium
6. child
8. wax
10. louse
11. pony
12. self
14. sheep
16. echo
17. gross
19. reef
21. patio
22. key
23. cod

Home Involvement Activity Make up small word-search puzzles that include irregular plurals, such as **geese** and **crises.** Write your words across, on a slant, or up and down. Then exchange and solve each other's puzzles.

Name _____

Read each group of words. Say and spell each word in bold type. Repeat the word. Then sort the words. Write each word in the correct box below.

- varieties of **wheat**
- danced the lively **waltzes**
- **wouldn't** want to stay
- cuts that need **stitches**
- a pair of **oxen**
- a **series** of steps
- sang sweet **melodies**
- **haven't** had lunch yet
- captured the **thieves**
- repairing the **chimneys**
- too many **crises**

- as her **injuries** heal
- **calves** in the meadow
- so **they'll** agree
- grazing **cattle**
- as **I've** always said
- **echoes** down the canyon
- if **we're** on time

Contractions	Plurals That Follow Rules	Irregular Plurals

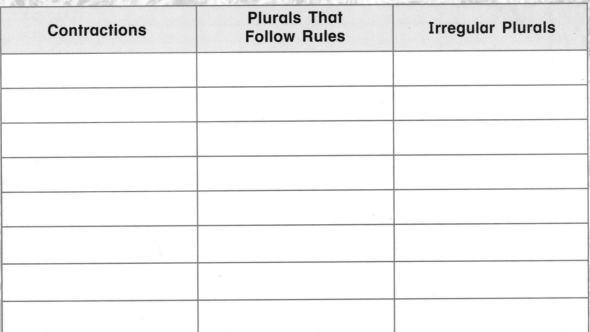

SPELL & WRITE

The Middle West has produced many great American writers. These writers were either born there or made the Midwest their home. Carl Sandburg, Willa Cather, Mark Twain, Ernest Hemingway, Laura Ingalls Wilder, and Mari Sandoz are six great writers whose names and works you may know. Like most good authors, these writers began writing about what they knew. In fact, many of them set their stories or poetry in the Midwest.

Now it's your turn to write about something you know. Write a personal narrative about an exciting adventure you have had. Use the people from the real-life experience and the actual setting. Include a logical sequence of events, and use the "I" point of view. Include at least two of these spelling words in your true story.

wheat	waltzes	wouldn't	stitches	oxen	series
melodies	haven't	thieves	chimneys	crises	injuries
calves	they'll	cattle	I've	echoes	we're

Willa Cather
(1873–1947)

Writer's Tips

As you revise, combine sentences to give more complete ideas. Then proofread your story for correct capitalization, punctuation, and spelling.

Speaker's Challenge

Use storytelling techniques to tell your story to your group or the class. Vary your tone of voice to emphasize a change of action in the plot. Speak loudly and clearly, and use appropriate gestures and body movement.

Carl Sandburg
(1878–1967)

Name _____

⭐ **Read about our nation's greatest river.
Then answer the questions that follow.**

Life Along the Mississippi River

Mark Twain, whose real name was Samuel Langhorne Clemens, often wrote about the Mississippi River. He once described it is a "wonderful book [with] a new story to tell every day."

The Native Americans who lived by the shores of the Mississippi were the first to tell the river's story. They used the river for traveling, hunting, and fishing. The river was the center of their lives.

When Thomas Jefferson made the Louisiana Purchase in 1803, the United States took ownership of the Mississippi River. Soon, new settlements followed. Later, riverboats came.

Steamboats brought another wave of change. These steam-powered giants could carry tons of goods to market. Steamboat traffic led to the rapid growth of cities along the river.

Mark Twain (1835–1910)

Early European explorers who mapped the river called it a "gathering of waters." Yet they could have called it a gathering of animals and people. Nearly half of North America's ducks, geese, and swans use the river as a migration path. More than 200 kinds of fish swim in its waters. Beaver, muskrats, otters, and turtles also make the river their home.

Millions of people also flock to the Mississippi River each year. These people are inspired by the new stories the river has to tell.

📖 **Reader's Response**

1. **What do you think Mark Twain meant by his description of the river?**

2. **How do you think steamboat traffic led to the growth of cities along the river?**

3. **Would you like to take a riverboat ride down the Mississippi River? Why? What do you think the trip would be like?**

Writers and artists who travel on the Mississippi are inspired by the beauty of the river. In fact, these people are often inspired by their natural surroundings. They may even form special attachments to mountains, oceans, forests, deserts, or plains. Indeed, they may create poems and paintings that show the beauty of something special in nature.

Describe something in nature that is special to you. Examples may include a canyon, a field, a mountain, or even a river. Write a vivid description of this natural feature and tell why you feel it is special. Use at least two of these words to describe.

majestic	wildlife	dramatic	silence	peaceful	magnificent
scenery	inspiring	breathtaking	beautiful	awesome	private

Writer's Tip

Use vivid verbs and adjectives to give your readers a mental picture of your description. Keep your audience in mind as you write.

_____

_____

_____

_____

_____

_____

_____

_____

_____

Writer's Challenge

Imagine the perfect photograph of the natural feature you have described. Now create the perfect caption for that photo. Use exact words and vivid language.

Scotts Bluff towers above the flat plains in Nebraska.

Name _____

Add s or es, ed, **and** ing **to each base word. Write the new words on the lines. Make spelling changes as needed.**

Base Word	Add s or es	Add ed	Add ing
1. arch	_____	_____	_____
2. talk	_____	_____	_____
3. fizz	_____	_____	_____
4. mix	_____	_____	_____
5. crash	_____	_____	_____
6. occur	_____	_____	_____
7. apply	_____	_____	_____
8. erase	_____	_____	_____

Write the base word for each word below.

9. brushed _____

10. admitting _____

11. scurrying _____

12. rallies _____

Gateway Memorial Arch in St. Louis, Missouri

Add ed or ing **to the base word in bold type to complete each sentence.**

give 13. Mom has been _____ arts-and-crafts classes to senior citizens.

cut 14. She is _____ up small fabric squares for a quilting project.

hurry 15. Last night, she _____ to class with a large box of stuffing.

stitch 16. The class watched as she _____ and filled part of a quilt.

display 17. All the students will be _____ their crafts at the fair.

Write the plural form of each word.

1. tax _____
2. roof _____
3. calf _____
4. deer _____
5. child _____
6. series _____
7. crisis _____
8. knife _____
9. ox _____
10. bush _____
11. man _____
12. wolf _____
13. potato _____
14. piano _____

Fill in the circle of the words that make up the contraction in bold type.

15. I **shouldn't** complain. ○ would not ○ should not ○ will not
16. **She'll** be surprised. ○ She all ○ She will ○ She would
17. **Who's** at the door? ○ Who is ○ Who has ○ Who was
18. **Let's** go swimming. ○ Let is ○ Let us ○ Let as
19. I **won't** argue. ○ could not ○ will not ○ would not

Underline the word that correctly completes each sentence. Then write the word on the line.

20. Many _____ serve good pizza, but Chicago's pizza stands alone.
    city   citys   cities

21. Chicago-style pizza is thick—two _____ thick in some cases!
    inchs   inch   inches

22. Deep-dish pizza is so gooey that people eat it with _____ and forks.
    knifes   knives   knifves

Extend & Apply

How do you like your pizza? Give your answer in a short paragraph.
Use at least one plural word and one contraction.

Name _____

Helpful Hint

Add an **apostrophe** and an **s** (**'s**) to the end of a singular noun to show who or what has or owns something.

the basketball belonging to Beth = Beth**'s** basketball

the challenges facing one champion = one champion**'s** challenges

the cell phone that James has = James**'s** cell phone

⭐ **Each of the following phrases is about one of Indiana's state record holders. Rewrite each phrase. Add 's to the word in bold type to show who or what has or owns something.**

1. the speed record set by a **turkey** _____

2. the best archer in **Muncie** _____

3. the first lighthouse in **Indiana** _____

4. the fastest elevator in the **state** _____

5. the gold medals won by that **swimmer** _____

6. the largest barn in this **county** _____

7. the biggest salad ever made in **Greenwood** _____

8. the 57-pound catfish caught by a **Hoosier** _____

⭐ **Write the possessive form of each word.**

9. student _____   10. staff _____

11. cyclist _____   12. editor _____

13. fox _____   14. country _____

15. teacher _____   16. boy _____

17. Ms. Kim _____   18. Charles _____

19. Pedro _____   20. brother _____

WORK TOGETHER

Work with a partner. Write five sentences that use the possessive form of a noun, but leave out the **apostrophe** and the **s** (**'s**). Exchange papers. Insert the **apostrophe** and the **s** (**'s**) correctly in each sentence.

Read the following phrases. Underline the ten phrases that show who or what has or owns something. Then write a sentence for each phrase you have underlined.

Fort Wayne's courthouse	three nights	the team's mascot
the mayor's plan	this city's nickname	a golfer's paradise
huge horse farms	creeks and streams	Dave's Dairy Barn
the town's location	highway repairs	the governor's idea
summer sunsets	Gus's tickets	the speedway's turns

1. _____

_____

2. _____

_____

3. _____

_____

4. _____

_____

5. _____

_____

6. _____

_____

7. _____

The **track**'s hairpin turns at the Indy 500

8. _____

_____

9. _____

_____

10. _____

_____

Home Involvement Activity Read together an article or a column from the sports pages of a newspaper. Circle each singular possessive noun that you find.

Name _____

Helpful Hints

Add only an **apostrophe** (') to form the **possessive** of a plural noun that ends in **s.**

the new ship of the owners = the owner**s'** new ship
the farm owned by her parents = her parent**s'** farm

Add an **apostrophe** and an **s** (**'s**) to form the possessive of a plural noun that does not end in **s.**

the bird that belongs to the children = the children**'s** bird
the vacation of the women = the women**'s** vacation

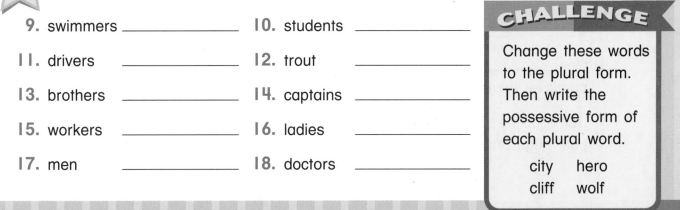

The Midwestern **state**s' busy waterways

⭐ **Rewrite each phrase. Add an apostrophe (') or an apostrophe and an s ('s) to the word in bold type to show who or what has or owns something.**

1. the cargo ships on the **lakes** _____

2. the sailboats of my **friends** _____

3. the fishing trip of our **teachers** _____

4. the tools of these **engineers** _____

5. the boat race for the **women** _____

6. the bicycles that belong to the **children** _____

7. the view from their **cabins** _____

8. the cameras of those **tourists** _____

⭐ **Write the possessive form of each word.**

9. swimmers _____ 10. students _____

11. drivers _____ 12. trout _____

13. brothers _____ 14. captains _____

15. workers _____ 16. ladies _____

17. men _____ 18. doctors _____

CHALLENGE

Change these words to the plural form. Then write the possessive form of each plural word.

city   hero
cliff   wolf

Read each phrase. If the words show that one person or thing has or owns something, write the word *one.* If the words show that more than one has or owns something, write *more than one.*

1. the forest rangers' lookout   _____

2. the leader's responsibilities   _____

3. the farmers' crops   _____

4. the sailors' voyage   _____

5. the city planner's new proposal _____

6. the guide's maps   _____

7. the calves' owner   _____

8. the parks' natural beauty   _____

South Dakota's Badlands National Park

Read the sentences about Badlands National Park. Underline the word that completes each sentence correctly. Then write the word on the line. Watch out! Don't confuse plurals and possessives.

9. This national _____ location is in southwestern South Dakota.   parks   park's   parks'

10. It has nearly 244,000 _____ of rock formations mixed with grass prairie.   acres   acre's   acres'

11. The park contains the _____ richest fossil beds from 23–35 million years ago.   worlds   world's   worlds'

12. Badlands National Park averages about

    1.1 million _____ each year.   visitors   visitor's   visitors'

13. The summers are hot and dry, and the

    _____ winters are usually cold.   Badlands'   Badland's   Badland

14. One _____ facilities are primitive; there is no running water.   camp's   camps   camps'

15. Some of the _____ take hikers past huge prairie dog towns.   trails   trail's   trails'

Home Involvement Activity Write one sentence each for the following pairs:
trails and **trail's**   **visitor's** and **visitors'**
rangers and **rangers'**

Name _____

Read each group of words. Say and spell each word in bold
type. Repeat the word. Then sort the words. Write each
word in the correct box below.

- strong **arguments**
- **aren't** going to win
- the **reporters'** coverage
- in the **editor's** column
- for the **country's** own good
- agree with their **viewpoints**
- if **you're** interested
- **won't** get their attention
- at a **women's** club

- to hold the **debates**
- closing **statements**
- what they **might've** said
- explain our **positions**
- get **supporters'** comments
- if **you'll** listen
- obeying the **official's** rules
- the **opponent's** remarks
- in the **speakers'** own words

Lincoln-Douglas debate, 1858

Singular Possessives

Plural Possessives

Plurals

Contractions

SPELL & WRITE

In the 1800s, Americans flocked to hear public speeches. Large crowds listened to readings, lectures, and debates. The audience would stay for hours to hear good speakers make sound arguments.

Abraham Lincoln held several famous debates with Stephen A. Douglas in 1858. Lincoln was running against Douglas in an Illinois state election. Both men were fine speakers. Both had strong ideas. Lincoln lost that election. Yet his great speeches against slavery won him national attention.

⭐ **Choose a topic that you feel strongly about. Write a persuasive speech. Present your main idea or argument in a strong topic sentence. Give convincing supporting details. Use at least two of these spelling words.**

> arguments   aren't   reporters'   editor's   country's   viewpoints
> you're   won't   women's   debates   statements   might've
> positions   supporters'   you'll   official's   opponent's   speakers'

Writer's Tip

Arguments are most convincing if you support them with facts. Don't rely on opinions alone to try to persuade your audience.

Speaker's Challenge

In formal debates, teams argue both sides of an issue. Yet team members cannot always represent the side in which they believe. Choose an issue. Plan arguments for the side you do *not* support. All the same, make your arguments strong and persuasive. Save your strongest argument for last.

Name _____

Helpful Hints

A **compound word** is made up of two or more smaller words.

back + pack = **backpack**   farm + land = **farmland**

Some compound words use hyphens.

drive-in   **mother-in-law**

Other compound words are two separate words.

control tower   **poison ivy**

Cleveland's busy **waterfront**

⭐ **Write the compound word described in each clue. Check a dictionary if you are not sure whether to write the compound as one word, as a word with a hyphen, or as two words.**

1. This ship travels in space. _____

2. You can dive off this board. _____

3. This shoe is used to walk on snow. _____

4. This building rises high into the sky. _____

5. This "dog" is served hot on a bun. _____

6. Here's a place to rest your foot. _____

7. He's the husband of your sister. _____

8. This bear lives in polar regions. _____

9. You might play on this ground. _____

⭐ **Underline the compound word in each phrase. Draw a line up and down to separate the two smaller words that make up the compound word.**

10. saw birds on a rooftop

11. waited for the countdown

12. slept in the bedroom

13. carrying a suitcase

14. mails a postcard

15. decided not to double-park

WORD STRATEGY

Divide an unfamiliar **compound word** into two smaller words when you read. This strategy will help you figure out the meaning and pronunciation of the word. Use this strategy to write definitions for these compound words:

footbridge
pathfinder

⭐ **Match a word from Column _A_ with a word from Column _B_ to build seven compound words. Write the compound words on the lines. Check a dictionary if you are not sure whether to write the compound as one word or two.**

A
roller
rain
spot
fire
honey
book
bee

1. _____

2. _____

3. _____

4. _____

5. _____

6. _____

7. _____

B
light
coaster
drill
comb
hive
bow
shelf

⭐ **Read the seven compound words that you wrote. Write a sentence for each word.**

8. _____

_____

9. _____

_____

10. _____

_____

11. _____

_____

12. _____

_____

13. _____

_____

14. _____

_____

Home Involvement Activity Work together to make a list of compound words that begin or end with **fire** and **light**. Your list may include **fire** engine, bon**fire**, **light**house, and candle**light**.

Name _____

Helpful Hints

Many **compound words** have more than two syllables. Look at the compound word **doubleheader.** How many syllables does the word have? Here's a way to figure it out.

First, separate the compound word into two smaller words.

doubleheader = double + header

Then count the number of syllables in each smaller word.

Dou/ble has 2 syllables.
Head/er has 2 syllables.
2 + 2 = 4

The compound word **doubleheader** has 4 syllables.

Divide each compound word into two smaller words. Write the two words. Count the number of syllables in each smaller word. Then add the number of syllables. The first one has been done for you.

Compound Word	Smaller Words		Syllables		
1. turtleneck	turtle	+ neck	2	+ 1	= 3
2. double-jointed	_____	+ _____	___	+ ___	= ___
3. motor scooter	_____	+ _____	___	+ ___	= ___
4. grasshopper	_____	+ _____	___	+ ___	= ___
5. summertime	_____	+ _____	___	+ ___	= ___

Underline the compound word in each phrase. Draw a line up and down to separate the compound word into syllables.

6. runs to home plate

7. watched the townspeople

8. drenched in the downpour

9. listens to the loudspeaker

10. took her raincoat

11. avoids the rattlesnakes

12. sees everybody at the game

13. plays in the afternoon

CHALLENGE

Write a sports paragraph that includes these four compound words:

baseball
doubleheader
left-handed
home run

LESSON 41: Compound Words and Syllables

85

Match a word from Column **A** with a word from Column **B** to form six compound words that name different kinds of food. Write the words on the lines. Then draw a line up and down to separate each compound "food" word into syllables.

A
lamb
water
grape
pop
blue
corn

1. _____

2. _____

3. _____

4. _____

5. _____

6. _____

B
corn
meal
berry
fruit
chop
melon

Play a food-naming game. Brainstorm with a group for five minutes to list ten compound food names. Then separate each compound word into two smaller words. Count the number of syllables in each word. Finally, add the total number of syllables of all the words.

Compound Words	Smaller Words	Syllables
7. _____	_____ + _____	___ + ___ = ___
8. _____	_____ + _____	___ + ___ = ___
9. _____	_____ + _____	___ + ___ = ___
10. _____	_____ + _____	___ + ___ = ___
11. _____	_____ + _____	___ + ___ = ___
12. _____	_____ + _____	___ + ___ = ___
13. _____	_____ + _____	___ + ___ = ___
14. _____	_____ + _____	___ + ___ = ___
15. _____	_____ + _____	___ + ___ = ___
16. _____	_____ + _____	___ + ___ = ___

Total: _____

LESSON 41: Compound Words and Syllables

Home Involvement Activity Brainstorm a list of imaginary compound food names. For example, would you like to drink a **meatball shake?** How about some **knuckleberry pie?** Create a menu of your funny foods.

Name _____

Read about an amazing artist who uses Midwestern farmland as his canvas. Then answer the questions that follow.

How to Grow a Painting

by Gail Skroback Hennessey

The Statue of Liberty in a wheat field in Kansas

Stan Herd isn't your everyday artist. His brush is a tractor, his canvas is the Earth and his paints are sunflowers and other plants!

Herd is a "crop artist." None of his "paintings" would fit on the wall of a museum. Take, for example, his picture of a sunflower in a vase. The sunflower is 150 feet long and the vase is 300 feet high. The painting sits in a field of Lawrence, KS. The sunflower is made of, well, sunflowers. The vase is green clover.

Herd got the idea to do crop art when he was flying over Kansas. Herd said, "I saw beautiful designs of the farmlands below. I thought, 'This is a wonderful art form for people who fly.'"

Herd can't just paint on the spur of the moment. He first spends a lot of time checking out the land he's going to use. Herd looks for running water that can destroy the work. He checks for chemicals in the ground that can change the colors of the field. He then flies above the field to get a better view of his "canvas." Next, Herd sits down and draws his picture on grid paper.

Once that's finished, Herd sticks bright orange flags in the ground. Each flag corresponds to a dot on his grid. Then he digs lines into the ground, connecting the flags. It's like a connect-the-dot drawing!

Herd digs with tractors, plows, rakes, hoes— even his feet. Then he checks his work. Says Herd, "Unlike most artists, who take a step back to inspect their paintings, I have to drive to the airport, get in a plane and fly above my painting!"

Reader's Response

1. **Describe "crop art." Why is it unusual?**

2. **What does Stan Herd do to create a work of crop art? Give the steps in order, from first to last.**

3. **Would you like to be a "crop artist"? Explain your reasons.**

LESSON 42: Connecting Reading and Writing
Comprehension—Sequence; Synthesize

87

Stan Herd follows a sequence of steps before he begins to create a piece of crop art. First, he tries to find a piece of land to use. Next, he checks for running water and for chemicals in the ground that can hurt his work. After that, he flies over the field to get a better view of his "canvas." Then, he draws his picture on grid paper.

Imagine you are going to create an interesting work of art. Your artwork might be a sculpture of "found" objects or a collage. Write a "how-to" paragraph of the steps you would take to create your artwork. Explain what you would do first, next, and finally. Use some of these time-order words.

first	next	then	finally	when	still	meanwhile	while
now	then	last	soon	later	before	during	after

_____

_____

_____

_____

_____

_____

_____

_____

Writer's Tips

• Arrange your steps in the best order.

• Combine shorter steps.

• Summarize your information at the end.

Speaker's Challenge

Present your writing as a "how-to" speech. Vary the tone of your voice to stress the important steps in the process. Use visual aids to help you explain.

Finny Fish sculpture by Alexander Calder, 1948

Name _____

⭐ **Write the plural form of each base word. Then write the possesive form of each plural word.**

1. radish _____ _____

2. statue _____ _____

3. monkey _____ _____

4. wife _____ _____

5. mouse _____ _____

⭐ **Rewrite each phrase. Use an apostrophe and an s ('s) or an apostrophe (') to show who or what has or owns something.**

6. the roar of that engine _____

7. the rattles that belongs to those babies _____

8. the mayor of this city _____

9. the badges that belong to the captains _____

10. the locker room meant for the women _____

11. the medals of those heroes _____

12. the feed for the animals _____

13. the books of these students _____

⭐ **Fill in the circle of the word that correctly completes each sentence. Then write the word on the line.**

14. The Middle West is known as our _____ breadbasket.
    ○ nation's   ○ nation   ○ nations'

15. _____ lives in the Corn Belt depend on their ability to grow corn.
    ○ Farmers   ○ Farmers'   ○ Farmer's

16. Here, on the flat land of the Great Plains, growing wheat and corn

    is a way of life for men, women, and _____.
    ○ children   ○ child's   ○ children's

Complete each sentence with a compound word. Write the word on the line.

Wheelchair race at Goodwill Games

1. A chair mounted on wheels

   is a _____.

2. Boats that you row

   are _____.

3. The way you send someone off on

   a trip is a _____.

Read the passage. For each numbered blank, there is a choice of words below. Fill in the circle of the word that completes the sentence correctly.

The National Road was built in **4**, starting in 1811. It was our **5** response to change. People were moving to the West in great numbers, and they needed a way to get there. By 1850, the National Road had reached Illinois. However, by then, the coming of the railroad had stopped **6** to extend the National Road. Much later, the old National Road became part of U.S. Highway 40.

4. ○ stage's   ○ stages   ○ stage

5. ○ country's   ○ countries   ○ countries'

6. ○ plan's   ○ plans'   ○ plans

Reread the passage. Circle the letter of each answer below.

7. Why was the National Road started?
   a. There were too many cars.
   b. People were moving to the West.
   c. Workers needed jobs.
   d. The railroad was coming.

8. How long did it take for the road to reach Illinois?
   a. more than a century
   b. nearly 11 years
   c. about 40 years
   d. less than 10 years

Extend & Apply

Suppose that you and your family wanted to drive from Maryland, where the National Road began, west to the Pacific Ocean. Use a road atlas to plan the route.

"Mountain Lying Down"

The Southwest is indeed a "land of enchantment." The Grand Canyon is just one of the wonders of the Southwest.

The Grand Canyon is 277 miles across. In some spots it is 10 miles wide. The Paiute call it *Kaibab*, or "Mountain Lying Down." To the Spanish explorers, it was *Gran Cañón*.

Native Americans knew about the Grand Canyon long before the first Europeans arrived in the 1500s. In about the year A.D. 500, the Anasazi came. They farmed the dry land and made baskets, pottery, and sandals. They lived in small villages in houses they built with stone. A thousand years later, these people were gone.

On the rim of the Grand Canyon are thick forests of aspen and fir. The temperatures there are cool. Much snow falls in the winter. Yet the floor of the canyon is a desert. It is hot and dry—and home to many different kinds of cacti. Because of the huge differences in elevation and moisture in the Grand Canyon, a wide variety of plants and animals can live there.

Today, more than 4 million people visit the Grand Canyon each year. You can be sure that most of these tourists leave with a new understanding of the word—*awesome!*

Critical Thinking

1. What is "awesome" about the Grand Canyon?

2. What was life like for the Anasazi who lived in the Grand Canyon area?

3. Have you ever been to the Grand Canyon? If so, what was it like? If not, would you like to go? Explain why.

Word Study at Home

Dear Family,

Your child has begun Unit 4 of Sadlier's *Word Study* program. Lessons in this unit focus on prefixes and suffixes and on how they change the meaning of the base words and roots that include them. The theme of this unit is the *Southwest*.

A **prefix** is a word part added to the beginning of a base word or root. Some common prefixes are **un-, re-, dis-, de-,** and **ex-.**

A **suffix** is a word part added to the end of a base word or root. Some common suffixes are **-ful, -less, -ness,** and **-ion.**

A **root** is the main part of a word. Roots become words when a prefix or a suffix is added to them. Add the prefix **ex-** ("out of") and the suffix **-ion** ("act or result of") to the root **-tract-** ("pull"): **ex- + -tract- + -ion = extraction.** This word means "the act of pulling out, as a tooth."

"Mountain Lying Down"

The Southwest is indeed a "land of enchantment." The Grand Canyon is just one of the wonders of the Southwest.

The Grand Canyon is 277 miles across. In some spots it is 10 miles wide. The Paiute call it *Kaibab*, or "Mountain Lying Down." To the Spanish explorers, it was *Gran Cañón*.

Native Americans knew about the Grand Canyon long before the first Europeans arrived in the 1500s. In about the year A.D. 500, the Anasazi came. They farmed the dry land and made baskets, pottery, and sandals. They lived in small villages in houses they built with stone. A thousand years later, these people were gone.

On the rim of the Grand Canyon are thick forests of aspen and fir. The temperatures there are cool. Much snow falls in the winter. Yet the floor of the canyon is a desert. It is hot and dry—and home to many different kinds of cacti. Because of the huge differences in elevation and moisture in the Grand Canyon, a wide variety of plants and animals can live there.

Today, more than 4 million people visit the Grand Canyon each year. You can be sure that most of these tourists leave with a new understanding of the word—awesome!

Critical Thinking

1. What is "awesome" about the Grand Canyon?
2. What was life like for the Anasazi who lived in the Grand Canyon area?
3. Have you ever been to the Grand Canyon? If so, what was it like? If not, would you like to go? Explain why.

LESSON 44: Introduction to Prefixes, Roots, Base Words, and Suffixes   91

Family Focus

- Create a Word Wall of prefixes and suffixes that your child will study in this unit. Add new words as they arise—in conversation or on the radio or television.

- Read together the nonfiction selection on page 91. Discuss it with your child. Has your family been to the Grand Canyon? Would your family like to visit this natural wonder? How would you get there from where you live?

LINKS TO LEARNING

To extend learning together, you might explore:

Web Sites
www.nps.gov/grca
www.johngregg.com

Video
The American Experience: Lost in the Grand Canyon, PBS Home Video.

Literature
Desert Dwellers: Native People of the American Southwest by Scott S. Warren ©1997.

Race to the Moonrise: An Ancient Journey by Sally Crum ©1998.

Name _____

Prefixes, **suffixes** and **roots** are word parts.
You can discover the meaning of a word
through its word parts.

HINT: You can add a prefix *or* a suffix *or*
both to a **base word** to form a new word
or change a word's meaning. For example,
read is the base word in **unreadable.**

⭐ **Write the base word that completes the sentence correctly.**

1. The base word in **refillable** is _____.   refill   fillable   fill

HINT: A **root** is the main part of a word. A root usually cannot stand alone.
Add a prefix *or* a suffix *or* both to a root to form a word. The root **pel**
means "drive." The prefix **ex** means "out." To **expel** is "to drive out."

⭐ **Write the root that completes the sentence correctly.**

2. The root in **injection** is _____.   in   ject   inject

HINT: A **prefix** is a word part added to the beginning of a base word or root.
The prefix in **disagree** is **dis. Dis** means "not." To **disagree** is "not to agree."

⭐ **Write the prefix that completes the sentence correctly.**

3. The prefix in **return** is _____.   re   turn   return

HINT: A **suffix** is a word part added to the end of a base
word or root. The suffix in **friendship** is **ship. Ship**
means "state." **Friendship** is "the state of being friends."

⭐ **Write the suffix that completes the sentence correctly.**

4. The suffix in **unhappiness** is _____.
   ness   happy   un

WORK TOGETHER

Work with a partner.
Brainstorm a list of
prefixes and suffixes
that you can add to
the following roots to
build words:

ject   port   tract

Use what you know about word parts. Write the prefix, the base word, and the suffix in each word.

	Prefix	Base Word	Suffix
1. unsuccessful	_____	_____	_____
2. cooperative	_____	_____	_____
3. reusable	_____	_____	_____
4. semimonthly	_____	_____	_____
5. encouragement	_____	_____	_____
6. nonpoisonous	_____	_____	_____
7. unreasonable	_____	_____	_____
8. disappearance	_____	_____	_____
9. incompletion	_____	_____	_____
10. disgraceful	_____	_____	_____

Write the prefix, the root, and the suffix in each word.

	Prefix	Root	Suffix
11. contraction	_____	_____	_____
12. respectful	_____	_____	_____
13. invisible	_____	_____	_____
14. description	_____	_____	_____
15. protractor	_____	_____	_____
16. producer	_____	_____	_____
17. subtraction	_____	_____	_____
18. importance	_____	_____	_____
19. rejection	_____	_____	_____
20. inventive	_____	_____	_____

LESSON 45: Base Words, Roots, Prefixes, and Suffixes

Home Involvement Activity Look for words in advertisements that have prefixes *or* suffixes *or* both. Make a list. Then circle the base word or root in the words that you find. Make a Word Wall of these words.

Name _____

Copyright © by William H. Sadlier, Inc. All rights reserved.

Helpful Hints

A **prefix** is a word part added to the **beginning** of a **base word**. Adding a prefix to a word can change the meaning of the word. It can also make a new word.

The **prefix un** means "not," as in **un**equal.
The **prefix re** means "again," as in **re**make, or "back," as in **re**pay.
The **prefix dis** means "not or opposite of," as in **dis**agree.
The **prefix de** means "from," as in **de**scribe, "off," as in **de**rail, "reverse," as in **de**frost, or "bring down," as in **de**value.

Some words seem to have prefixes but do not. For example, when you remove the **un** from **under,** no base word remains.

The sentences below are about Arizona's Kitt Peak National Observatory. Complete each sentence by adding the prefix un, re, dis, or de to the base word in parentheses. Be sure the new word is spelled correctly.

CHALLENGE

Each of the following words has two prefixes. Underline both prefixes. Then tell a partner what each word means.

rediscovered
unrestrained

1. Astronomers took three years to _____ 149 other Southwestern peaks before they chose Kitt Peak as the place for an observatory. **(qualify)**

2. The observatory's 21 telescopes help scientists to

   _____ some of the mysteries of our vast universe. **(lock)**

3. The telescopes are aimed at distant stars and galaxies and can predict when certain events will happen again,

   or _____. **(occur)**

4. The scientists use computers that

   can _____ complex information. **(code)**

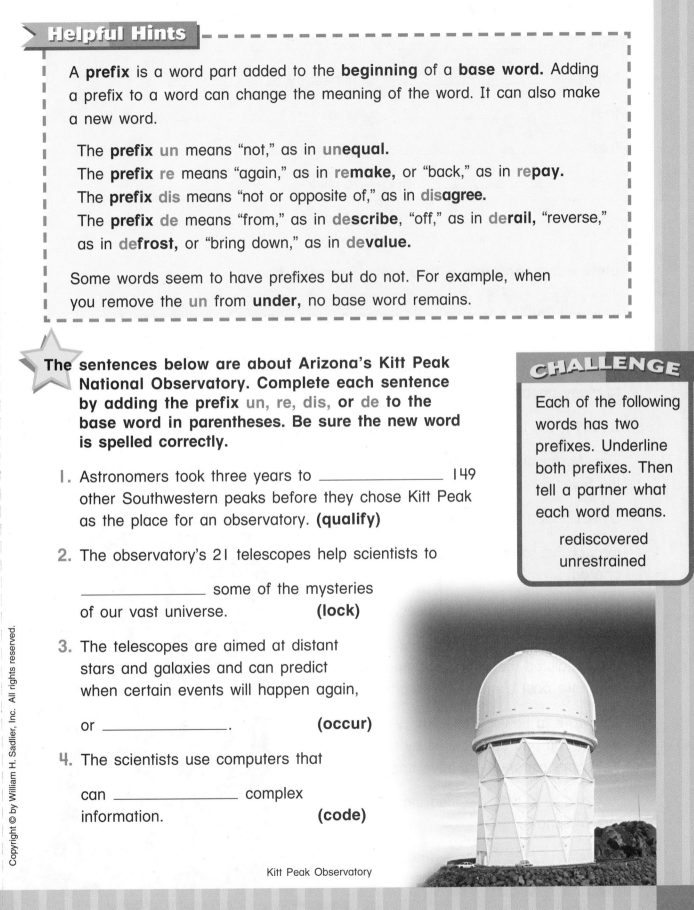

Kitt Peak Observatory

⭐ **Add un, re, dis, or de to each of the following base words. Write the new word on the line.**

1. think _____

2. live _____

3. happy _____

4. honest _____

5. fault _____

6. please _____

7. frost _____

8. apply _____

9. loyal _____

10. familiar _____

11. regard _____

12. elect _____

⭐ **Complete each sentence with a word from the box.**

| unpolluted | repaid | discover | unknown | disagree |

13. The achievements of the astronomer Percival Lowell may be _____ to many people.

14. In 1894, Dr. Lowell built an observatory in Flagstaff, Arizona. He knew that

    Flagstaff's cloudless skies and _____ air would be ideal for studying the Solar System.

15. Lowell hoped that his many hours of looking

    through his telescope would be _____ one day.

16. In 1930, a worker at the observatory was the

    first to _____ the planet Pluto. Lowell had predicted that there was another planet out there past Uranus and Neptune.

17. The work at Lowell Observatory has been recognized and appreciated by astronomers. Yet some astronomers have begun to

    _____ with the idea that Pluto is in fact a planet.

Telescope at Lowell Observatory

LESSON 46: Prefixes **un-, re-, dis-, de-**

Home Involvement Activity *The Return of the Pink Panther* is a movie that has a prefix in its title. What other movies have the prefix un, re, dis, or de in their names? Make a list together.

Name _____

Helpful Hints

The **prefix pre** means "before."

Children attend **pre**school before kindergarten.

The **prefix post** means "after."

A **post**script is an extra note placed after the end of a signed letter. Its abbreviation is P.S.

The **prefix ex** means "out of or from."

To **ex**claim is "to cry out."

The **prefix out** means "outside" or "greater than."

To **out**number is to have a greater number.

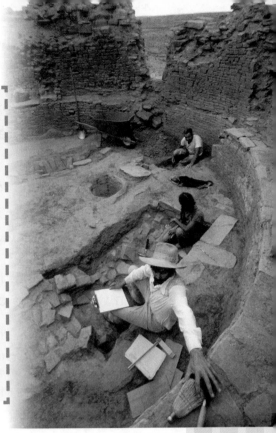

Archaeologists at an Anasazi ruin

Complete each sentence with a word from the box.

precautions	outweigh	prehistoric

1. Throughout the Southwest, _____ peoples, like the Anasazi, left evidence of the lives they had led long ago.

2. Archaeologists take great _____ so as not to disturb the remains of past cultures.

3. Usually, their findings _____ their efforts.

Underline the prefix in each word. Then use what you know about prefixes to write the meaning of the word on the line. Use a dictionary, if needed.

4. postdate _____

5. exchange _____

6. preplan _____

7. outlast _____

CHALLENGE

Pre and **post** are prefixes used to describe periods in time. For example, **pre-Columbian** means "before the arrival of Columbus in the Americas." Write the meaning of these words:

prewar

postwar

Choose a word from the box to answer each question correctly. Write the word on the line.

postpone	prejudge	exclaim	preface	exhale
outburst	preview	outskirts	exclude	exchange

1. Which word means "a showing of something ahead of time"? _____

2. Which word means "to cry out, as in surprise"? _____

3. Which word means "introduction to a book, often written by the author"? _____

4. Which word means "the area at the edge of a town or city"? _____

5. Which word means "to give or take one thing in return for another"? _____

6. Which word means "to pass judgment before knowing all the facts"? _____

7. Which word means "to keep out"? _____

8. Which word means "a bursting forth"? _____

9. Which word means "to breathe out"? _____

10. Which word means "to put off until later"? _____

Write a sentence for six of the words you wrote above.

11. _____

12. _____

13. _____

14. _____

15. _____

16. _____

LESSON 47: Prefixes **pre-, post-, ex-, out-**

Home Involvement Activity Write the four prefixes from this lesson, each on an index card. Shuffle the cards and place them face-down. Take turns picking cards. Build two words from the prefix on each card.

Name _____

Helpful Hints

Sub is a **prefix** that means "under" or "less than."

A **sub**marine is a ship that can go underwater.
The **sub**plot of a play or novel is less important than the main plot.

Trans is a **prefix** that means "across," "beyond," or "through."

The first **trans**continental railroad sped across the country in 1869.
Translucent material, like frosted glass, lets light pass through.

Underline the prefix in each word.

1. transport
2. subcommittee
3. transatlantic
4. subtitle
5. transform
6. subfreezing
7. submerge
8. subtopic
9. transplant
10. transmit
11. transform
12. subway

The Last Spike by Thomas Hill

Read each clue. Then unscramble the letters to form the word that fits the clue. Write the word on the line. All the words appear in the list above.

13. a title that usually explains the main title — **ubslitte** _____

14. across the Atlantic Ocean — **citlantarants** _____

15. a committee acting under the main committee — **mostbeeticum** _____

16. move a plant from one pot to another — **sanntpralt** _____

17. topic under the main topic — **busoptic** _____

18. underground train — **swabyu** _____

CHALLENGE

Use what you know about American history and the prefix **trans** to write the meaning of this statement:
*The **transcontinental** railroad linked the East and the West.*

The **prefix** **semi** means "half" or "partly."

Semisweet chocolate is partly sweet and partly bitter.

The **prefix** **mid** means "in the middle of."

Our **mid**winter sale starts in early February.

Underline the prefix in each word in the box below. Then complete each sentence with a word from the box. Use a word only once.

midweek	semicircle	midterm	midyear	semicolon	semiprivate
semiprecious	midway	semifinal	midtown	semiformal	

1. Chicago is _____ between New York and Los Angeles.

2. Our team lost in the _____ round of the play-off.

3. We always schedule our _____ checkup in June.

4. At a _____ dinner, a man would wear a suit, not a tuxedo.

5. We sat in a _____ around the fireplace.

6. We call the _____ special in our cafeteria the "Wednesday Surprise."

7. The central part of a city between its uptown and downtown areas is known as _____.

8. We are having a _____ exam on everything we have studied since the beginning of the fall term.

9. Turquoise is a _____ gem. It is not as valuable as a diamond or a ruby, but it is more valuable than a plain rock.

10. A _____ is a punctuation mark that is less final than a period, but greater than the pause for a comma.

11. A _____ hospital room is shared by two patients.

Turquoise—a **semi**precious stone

100

LESSON 48: Prefixes **sub-, trans-, mid-, semi-**

Home Involvement Activity Find out the names and features of some **semi**precious gems. Does anyone in your family have jewelry made from these stones? If so, create a display and exhibit cards to share.

Name _____

> **Helpful Hints**

The **prefixes** in, il, im, and ir mean "not."

incomplete = not complete   **im**possible = not possible

illogical = not logical   **ir**regular = not regular

The **prefixes** in and im appear before many different base words and roots.
The **prefix** il goes before words that begin with l.
The **prefix** ir goes before words that begin with r.

Underline the prefix in each word. Then on the line, use what you know about prefixes and base words to write the meaning of the word.

1. illegal _____

2. impolite _____

3. irresponsible _____

4. impatient _____

5. illiterate _____

6. inaccurate _____

7. impractical _____

8. insensitive _____

9. illegible _____

10. insincere _____

11. immortal _____

12. incorrect _____

13. impure _____

14. immature _____

15. irrelevant _____

16. inactive _____

WORD STRATEGY

To figure out the meaning of an unfamiliar word with a prefix, cover the prefix and read the rest of the word. Try that strategy with these words:

impartial
inability

Discuss how using the strategy helped you figure out the meaning of the words.

Read each passage. Then on the lines, write the answer to each question.

New Mexican painting by
Georgia O'Keeffe, 1941

1. Georgia O'Keeffe (1887–1986) was a great American artist. As a young child, she showed a strong talent for art. She felt **impatient** to grow up. She couldn't wait to become an artist.

   Why was the young Georgia O'Keeffe **impatient?** _____

   _____

2. Georgia O'Keeffe was born in Wisconsin and grew up on a farm. After she finished high school, she went to art school. She lived in New York City and in Chicago. Yet deep in her heart, she felt **incapable** of adjusting to city life. She longed for open space and clear light.

   Why did Georgia O'Keeffe feel **incapable** of living in a city? _____

   _____

3. Later on, New Mexico became O'Keeffe's home. She loved the clear light, fresh air, and freedom. She was a fiercely **independent** woman. She did not rely on others. She loved to hike, to spend time alone, and to paint.

   In what ways was O'Keeffe **independent?** _____

   _____

4. The images in O'Keeffe's artwork are bold and clear. O'Keeffe felt that bright light was **indispensable** to the creation of her lifelike art. She could not paint without it.

   What does **indispensable** mean? _____

   _____

5. When she was in her late seventies, O'Keeffe's eyesight began to fail. This change had an **irreversible** effect on her life as a painter. With great sadness, she had to give up painting.

   What had an **irreversible** effect on Georgia O'Keeffe? _____

   _____

Home Involvement Activity Talk with family members about the meaning of the words **mature** and **immature.** Discuss the opportunities available to students when they show they are mature.

Name _____

Helpful Hint

The **prefixes** co and com or con mean "with or together."

co exist = exist with   com pile = gather and put together
con join = join together

⭐ **Read each phrase below. Underline the word that has the prefix co, com, or con. Then circle the prefix in the word.**

1. a crowded airport concourse

2. compiles a list of names

3. composes a song about Texas

4. performs at a rock concert

5. one of the two cosigners

6. confirms the answer

7. concedes victory to the other team

8. will confront the issue

An airport con course

⭐ **Answer each question. Use a word from the box below. Write the word on the line.**

concurrent   compare   cooperate   combine

9. Which word means "happening at the same time"? _____

10. Which word means "to join or mix together"? _____

11. Which word means "to work together for a common purpose"? _____

12. Which word means "to examine together"? _____

WORK TOGETHER

Work with a group to brainstorm words that begin with the prefixes co, com, or con. Then scramble the letters of each word. Write each scrambled word on an index card. Take turns unscrambling the words.

The **prefixes** en and em have the same meaning.
En and **em** mean "to put into or on."

   encode   enforce   enjoy   embalm

The **prefixes** en and em may also mean "to cause to be or make."

   enable   enrich   enslave   embitter

En and **em** also mean "to cover or surround."

   encircle   enclose   entangle   embrace

You know that the **prefixes** in and im mean "not."
They also mean "in, into, within, or on."

   insight = can see into   import = bring in

Carlsbad Caverns

New Mexico is called the "Land of Enchantment."
Some of the enchantment happens underground.
Underline the word that best completes each
sentence about Carlsbad Caverns National Park.
Then write the word on the line.

1	Every year, about 750,000 people travel to southeastern New Mexico to _____ a fantastic experience.	inhale enlarge enjoy
2	Visitors to Carlsbad Caverns can _____ an underground world of rarely seen treasures within 75 caves.	engulf include inspect
3	Cave visitors will not _____ themselves if they stay on the trails and listen to the park rangers who guide them.	employ endanger enrage
4	Daring cave explorers can _____ themselves in a more adventurous cave experience.	immerse encounter embody
5	Adventurers actually _____ the opportunity to crawl through an underground wilderness of newly found caves.	encircle embrace inscribe

Home Involvement Activity Discuss the features of
a place that might earn the description "enchanted."
Talk about enchanting places that you have visited
together. What made them charming or enchanting?

Read each group of words. Say and spell each word in bold type. Repeat the word. Then sort the words. Write each word in the correct box below.

- **combine** business with pleasure

- **cooperate** with the police

- **displease** his family

- that we should **embrace**

- **enforce** the law

- an **illegal** contract

- an **impolite** remark

- an **irresponsible** act

- **inhale** pollution

- a **midseason** sale

- **outlasted** its usefulness

- **postdated** the check

- the **preface** to her book

- **reelect** her to another term

- in a **semiprivate** room

- added a funny **subtitle**

- in **unfamiliar** territory

- **transform** our government

Senate Room of Texas State Capitol

Words with **Two Syllables**	Words with **Three Syllables**	Words with **Four or More Syllables**

SPELL & WRITE

Barbara Jordan (1936–1996) was one of our nation's greatest speakers and defenders of the Constitution. She represented the people of Texas with "a will of iron and a voice of gold." Barbara was determined to get a good education. She worked to be strong and independent. With her eloquent voice, she spoke out for causes in which she believed.

Choose an issue that you feel strongly about, such as saving the environment. Write a short persuasive speech to your classmates. Try to get your audience to agree with your opinions and point of view. Use at least two of these spelling words in your speech.

combine	cooperate	displease	embrace	enforce	illegal
impolite	irresponsible	inhale	midseason	outlasted	postdated
preface	reelect	semiprivate	subtitle	unfamiliar	transform

_____

_____

_____

_____

_____

_____

_____

_____

> **Writer's Tip**
>
> Use the 5 steps of the writing process: prewrite, write, revise, proofread, and publish.

Barbara Jordan speaking in 1992

Speaker's Challenge

Learn more about the life of Barbara Jordan. Then give an oral report about this great American. Write your main ideas and important facts on note cards. Practice using your note cards before giving your report. Also practice pacing your speech.

Name _____

Add the prefix dis to two of the following base words. Add the prefix re to the two other words. Write the meaning of each new word.

Base Word	Word with Prefix	Meaning of New Word
1. cover	_____	_____
2. appear	_____	_____
3. apply	_____	_____
4. please	_____	_____

Add the prefix out to two of the following base words. Add the prefix pre to the two other words. Write the meaning of each new word.

Base Word	Word with Prefix	Meaning of New Word
5. caution	_____	_____
6. last	_____	_____
7. historic	_____	_____
8. burst	_____	_____

Add the prefix sub to one of the following base words. Add the prefix trans to the other word. Write the meaning of each new word.

Base Word	Word with Prefix	Meaning of New Word
9. plant	_____	_____
10. merge	_____	_____

Add the prefix il to one of the following base words. Add the prefix ir to the other base word. Write the meaning of each new word.

Base Word	Word with Prefix	Meaning of New Word
11. responsible	_____	_____
12. legal	_____	_____

Fill in the circle of the word that best completes each sentence. Then write the word on the line.

1. Do you picture Arizona as a desert? Well, the Grand Canyon State

   also has _____ mountain ski areas and snow-shoeing trails.
   ○ defrosted   ○ unspoiled   ○ impossible

2. Our family is taking a(n) _____ ski trip to Arizona.
   ○ midwinter   ○ postwar   ○ exchange

3. Maybe our trip will _____ with a lunar eclipse. If it does,
   we will watch it at the Lowell Observatory in Flagstaff.
   ○ discover   ○ engulf   ○ coincide

4. We'll also pan for _____ stones in one of Arizona's streams.
   ○ outnumbered   ○ semiformal   ○ semiprecious

Complete each sentence by combining a prefix with a base word in the box to form a new word. Write the new word on the line.

Prefixes

de

dis

en

out

Base Words

large

lasted

parted

satisfied

The southeastern corner of Arizona was once a busy mining region. The land held silver and copper. Miners found great veins of these valuable metals. Once word got out, miners and fortune hunters hurried there. Eager bosses hired cheap workers to help them strike it rich. Miners quickly built "boom

towns." They dreamed of how they would (5) _____ their cash boxes. Indeed, a few bosses got very rich. Yet most

failed and left (6) _____.

When the boom ended, the miners (7) _____. They left behind houses, shops, schools, and even jails. Some

abandoned houses have (8) _____ the miners who once lived in them. Today, in towns such as Gleeson, Pearce, and Cochise, visitors can see the "ghost towns" that remain.

Extend & Apply

Find out more about the old mining towns of the Southwest. Write a paragraph about one of these towns. Use at least two words that have prefixes.

Abandoned mining town in Arizona

Name _____

Helpful Hints

A **root** is the main part of a word. Roots have meaning, but few can stand alone. Roots become words when **prefixes** or **suffixes** are added to them. If you know the meaning of a root, you can often figure out the meaning of a word.

The **root pos** means "put or place."

To **depos**it is "to put money in a bank."

The **root pel** means "push" or "drive."

To re**pel** is "to drive back."

The **root tract** means "pull, draw back, or drag."

A **tract**or is a farm vehicle that pulls heavy loads.

The **root ject** means "throw" or "force."

To re**ject** is "to throw back."

The **root port** means "carry."

To ex**port** is "to carry goods out of one country to sell in another."

⭐ **Underline the root in each numbered word below. Then match each word with its meaning. Write the letter of the correct definition on the line.**

_____ 1. opposite a. to draw to or pull toward

_____ 2. expel b. the way a person or thing is placed

_____ 3. portfolio c. to drive out by force

_____ 4. position d. to draw away attention

_____ 5. attract e. placed at the other end or side

_____ 6. projector f. a machine that throws an image onto a screen

_____ 7. import g. a case for carrying loose papers or drawings

_____ 8. distract h. to bring in or carry goods from another country

WORK TOGETHER

Work with a partner to look through a newspaper or a book to find words formed from the roots given in this lesson. Make a list of the words that you find. Then exchange your list with the list prepared by another partner team.

⭐ **Choose the best word from the box to complete each sentence. Write the word on the line.**

compel	dispel	expose	portable	positive
propel	reject	retract	traction	transport

1. Mules have dependable _____. This makes them well suited for the rugged canyons of the Southwest, like those in the Grand Canyon.

2. These pack animals can safely

   _____ people and equipment up and down steep and winding trails.

3. People experienced in the outdoors hope

   to _____ the idea that it is too dangerous to hike in the desert. They know the importance of bringing a good supply of water, high-energy food, and sunscreen.

4. The intense desert heat should

   _____ any hiker to bring along a full canteen.

Mule riders above the Grand Canyon

5. With their _____ tent and lightweight gear, some hikers make their way down to the canyon floor for an overnight stay.

6. Because of a late start, some hikers have to _____ their original plan.

7. Some adventurers _____ themselves to the dangers (and excitement!) of white-water rafting.

8. The knowing guides _____, or draw back, the oars when the boats reach the rapids.

9. The rushing water will _____ the boats forward.

10. Plan your trip carefully. Know what to expect and what to take with you. If you respect the desert environment, you are more

    likely to have a _____ outdoor experience.

LESSON 53: Roots
-pos-, -pel-, -tract-, -ject-, -port-

Home Involvement Activity Brainstorm a list of words that have the roots in this lesson. Then take turns telling a cumulative story, one sentence at a time, about a family adventure. Use words from your list.

Name _____

Ped or Pod, ven or vent, and duc or duct are **roots**.

Ped or pod means "foot."

A **bi**ped is a two-footed animal.

Ven or vent means "come."

A **con**vent**ion** is a meeting where people come together.

Duc or duct means "lead" or "bring."

An **aque**duct is a pipe that brings water over a long distance.

Write the root that will complete the name of each picture.

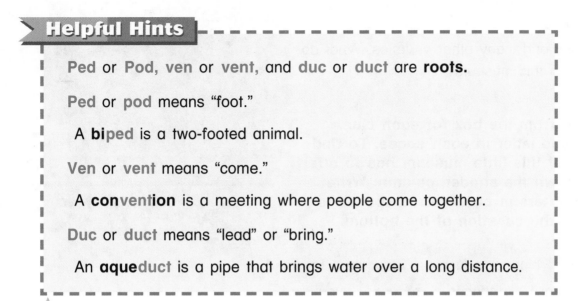

1 _ _ _ estrian	2 _ _ _ ium	3 re _ _ _ _ ion
4 con _ _ _ _ or	5 _ _ _ al	6 in _ _ _ _ ion

Write a word from the box below to complete each sentence.

adventure	conductors	introduced

7. Oklahoma _____ people to oil wells. Many people in the state became rich from the oil found on their land.

8. _____ on transcontinental railroads collected tickets.

9. Later, the automobile made driving a family _____.

CHALLENGE

Write one sentence for each of the six words shown in the pictures at the top of the page. Share your sentences with classmates.

The small Panhandle town of McLean, Texas, is home to the Devil's Rope Museum. On display there are Mack's twist, Billings' simple 4-point, Corsican clip, and many other varieties. What do you think is in this museum?

Use a word from the box for each clue. Write one letter in each space. To find out what this little museum has to offer, read down the shaded column. Write those letters in order in the spaces to answer the question at the bottom.

biped   bipod   educate   inductee   invent
pedestal   producer   reduce   ventured

1. like a tripod, but a two-legged stand   _ _ _ _ _

2. a base on which a statue stands   _ _ _ _ _ _ _ _

3. a person who brings people and money together to make a movie, TV series, or play   _ _ _ _ _ _ _ _

4. an animal that has two feet   _ _ _ _ _

5. to bring knowledge to people   _ _ _ _ _ _ _

6. someone who is brought into military service   _ _ _ _ _ _ _ _

7. to come up with something new   _ _ _ _ _ _

8. to bring down in size or value   _ _ _ _ _ _

9. "Nothing ___, nothing gained."   _ _ _ _ _ _ _ _

Question: What does the Devil's Rope Museum collect and exhibit?

Answer: _ _ _ _ _ _   W_ _ _

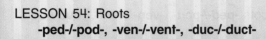
Home Involvement Activity What is the most unusual museum, exhibit, or collection you have ever seen or heard about? What idea do you have for a museum? Discuss your ideas.

Name _____

> **Helpful Hints**

Spect, **vid** or **vis**, **audi**, and **phon** are **roots**.

Spect and **vid** or **vis** all mean "see."

To **in**spect is to look at closely.
A **vid**eo is a recording you can see.
Vision is your sense of sight.

Audi or **audio** means "hear."

An **audi**ence is a group of listeners.

Phon, **phone**, or **phono** means "sound."

Phonics uses the sounds of letters to help you read.

An **audio**logy test to check hearing

⭐ **Read each definition. Then find the word in the box that matches it. Write that word on the line. Circle its root.**

audiometer	auditorium	evident	respect	spectacular
suspect	symphony	telephone	television	visit

1. to regard highly _____

2. a machine that measures your hearing _____

3. a hand-held device that carries sound _____

4. to look at with doubt or distrust _____

5. relating to a remarkable sight _____

6. to go to see someone or something _____

7. an orchestra or a harmony of sounds _____

8. a box for receiving pictures _____

9. easy to see or understand _____

10. a room or hall for an audience _____

> **CHALLENGE**

Use what you know about roots, music, and art to write the meaning of these words:

phonograph
spectrum

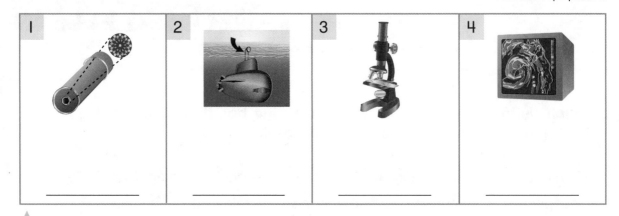

Helpful Hint

The **root** scope means "seeing or looking."

A **tele**scope is an instrument used for looking at the planets and stars.

⭐ **Identify each picture below.**
Find its name in the yellow box.
Then write the word on the line.

> microscope   radarscope   periscope   kaleidoscope

Kaleidoscope patterns

1	2	3	4
_____	_____	_____	_____

⭐ **Each item pictured above lets you look at or see things in a special way.**
Write a sentence about each of the four items. Describe what each one
is or does. If you need help, check a dictionary or an encyclopedia.

5. _____

_____

6. _____

_____

7. _____

_____

8. _____

_____

LESSON 55: Roots -spect-, -vid-/-vis-,
-audi-, -phon-, -scope-

Home Involvement Activity Discuss the following words: audition, evidence, phonics, revision, and spectacle. Explain how knowing the root of the word helps you understand its meaning.

Name _____

Helpful Hints

Scrib or Script, graph or gram, and log are **roots.**

Both scrib and script mean "write."

A prescription is a doctor's written directions for using medicine.
To **scribble** is to write carelessly or quickly.

The root **graph** means "something that writes or records."
The root **gram** means "something written or recorded."

A telegraph is a system for sending messages by wire.
A telegram is a message sent by **telegraph.**

The root **log** means "word or speech." Sometimes, this root is spelled as **logue.**

A **dialogue** is a conversation.

⭐ **Read the sentences. Underline the words that have the roots** scrib/script, graph/gram, **or** log.

1. The photograph of the Alamo on the cover of the book showed how the fort used to look.

2. In the prologue, the author told what had inspired her to write the book.

3. The monologue on the tape is clear and interesting.

4. I found the diagram of the fort very helpful.

5. The author's description of the battle is exciting.

6. My copy of the book has the writer's autograph in it.

7. However, she scribbled her signature.

8. The author's apology included all the people she had forgotten to thank.

CHALLENGE

The roots graph/gram and log are words by themselves. What does each word mean? Write a sentence for each word. Do any of the words match the meaning of the root?

The Alamo in San Antonio, Texas

⭐ **Read each phrase. Underline the root in each word in bold type.**

1. **prescribed** rest and relaxation
2. the **dialogue** in the novel
3. a 1-year **subscription** to that magazine
4. **graphite** in the pencil
5. read the **inscription** on the rock
6. uses perfect **grammar**
7. used **logic** to solve the problem
8. was very **apologetic**

⭐ **Write an original sentence for each of the eight words in bold type above. Use a dictionary, if needed.**

9. _____
_____

10. _____
_____

11. _____
_____

12. _____
_____

13. _____
_____

14. _____
_____

15. _____
_____

16. _____
_____

Car "sculptures" in Texas

LESSON 56: Roots
-scrib-/-script-, -graph-/-gram-, -log-

Home Involvement Activity Suppose you could put a large original sculpture in front of your home. What would it be? Brainstorm to create a list of ideas. What did you decide? Write a **description**.

Name _____

> ## Helpful Hints

The **root** fac means "to make or do." It comes from the Latin word *facere.*

In English, this root is spelled in many ways, including fac, fact, fec, fect, fic, fit, and fy. This root can appear at the beginning, in the middle, or at the end of a word.

fact   ef**fect**   **fic**tion   bene**fit**   rati**fy**

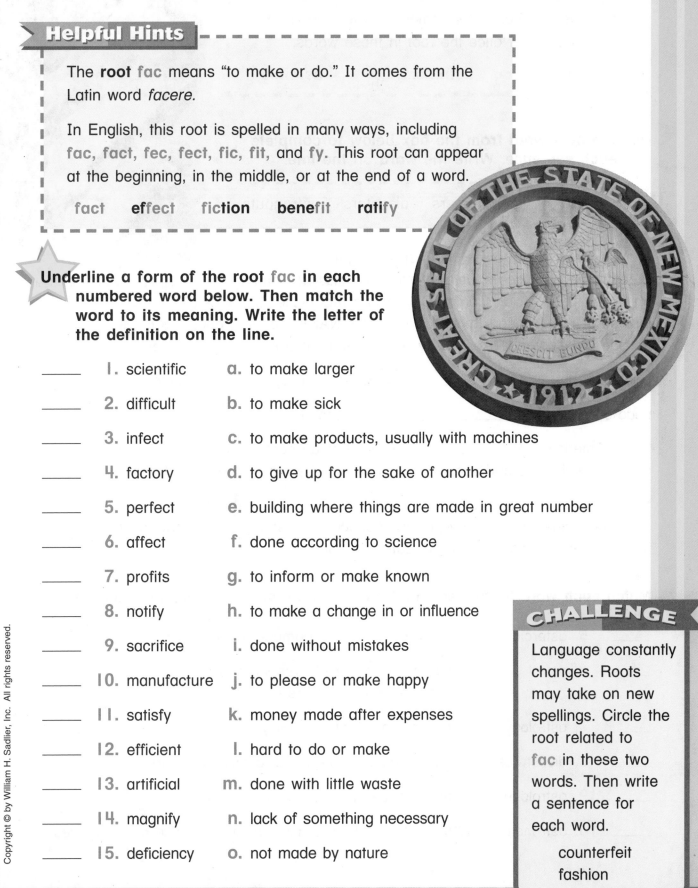

Underline a form of the root fac **in each numbered word below. Then match the word to its meaning. Write the letter of the definition on the line.**

_____	1. scientific	**a.** to make larger
_____	2. difficult	**b.** to make sick
_____	3. infect	**c.** to make products, usually with machines
_____	4. factory	**d.** to give up for the sake of another
_____	5. perfect	**e.** building where things are made in great number
_____	6. affect	**f.** done according to science
_____	7. profits	**g.** to inform or make known
_____	8. notify	**h.** to make a change in or influence
_____	9. sacrifice	**i.** done without mistakes
_____	10. manufacture	**j.** to please or make happy
_____	11. satisfy	**k.** money made after expenses
_____	12. efficient	**l.** hard to do or make
_____	13. artificial	**m.** done with little waste
_____	14. magnify	**n.** lack of something necessary
_____	15. deficiency	**o.** not made by nature

> ## CHALLENGE

Language constantly changes. Roots may take on new spellings. Circle the root related to fac in these two words. Then write a sentence for each word.

counterfeit

fashion

Helpful Hint

The root **astro** or **aster** comes from the Greek word for "star." Notice the root in these words.

astronaut   **astro**nomy   **aster**oid

Astro**naut** at Johnson Space Center

Use the best word from the box below to complete each sentence. Write the word on the line.

> asterisk   astronomers   disasters   astronauts

You have seen movies about space flight. You have probably heard space travelers talking to "Mission Control" on Earth. The Mission Control Center is a real place. It is located at the Johnson Space Center. This NASA facility is about 25 miles outside of Houston, Texas. Many engineers, mathematicians, computer

scientists, and **(1)**_____ work there. They work in teams to

head off **(2)**_____ before they happen.

All American **(3)**_____ are trained here. They must learn to use high-tech tools and space-age instruments before they get the "okay"

to go into space. You may see an **(4)**_____ next to the name of some Americans who have flown in space. This star-shaped mark shows that the person was not a NASA astronaut, but a guest aboard a flight.

Match each word to its meaning. Write the letter of the definition on the line.

_____ 5. asteroid   **a.** causing great loss, damage, or suffering

_____ 6. astral   **b.** any of the minor planets with orbits between those of Mars and Jupiter

_____ 7. astrology   **c.** relating to the stars; starry

_____ 8. disastrous   **d.** an instrument once used to measure stars

_____ 9. astrolabe   **e.** the science of the planets and stars

_____ 10. astronomy   **f.** the belief that stars and planets influence people's lives

Home Involvement Activity The Latin root *stella* means "star," as in con**stella**tion. Work together to figure out the meaning of **stellar** and **stelliform**. Then write a sentence for each word.

Name _____

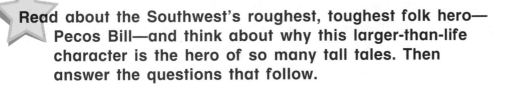

Read about the Southwest's roughest, toughest folk hero—
Pecos Bill—and think about why this larger-than-life
character is the hero of so many tall tales. Then
answer the questions that follow.

Rough, Tough Pecos Bill

by Lester David

When cowboys of the late 1800's
gathered in bunkhouses at the end of
the day, the talk naturally turned to
Pecos Bill. This mythical cowpoke was
the roughest, toughest and best range
rider in the Southwest.

The smartest, too. He invented
roping and Western movies. He even
taught broncos how to buck. He taught
his own horse so well that no man—
except Bill—could ride him. That's why
Bill named him Widow Maker.

During a long dry spell, Bill trekked
to the Gulf of Mexico to carry water to
his parched home state of Texas. Tiring
of the long journey, he decided instead
to dig a little trench for the water. The
result? The Rio Grande, the river that
forms Texas' southern border.

But that dig was nothing compared
with the Grand Canyon. Yep, Pecos Bill
dug that, too. When a terrific urge to
mine for gold struck him one day, he
started digging. Before he could yell
"Eureka!" he had created the canyon.

Wild stories abound about how his
days ended. The best yarn: Bill took
one look at a city slicker from the East
and just laughed himself to death!

Reader's Response

1. Name one problem that Pecos Bill tried
to solve. What happened as a result?

2. Do you think that Pecos Bill was a
real person? Could he have done
the things that the stories say he
did? Explain.

3. Some heroes of tall tales were real
people. Yet the stories about them
grew taller each time they were told.
Why do you think this happened?

Folk heroes like Paul Bunyan, John Henry, Davy Crockett, Annie Oakley, and Pecos Bill all had one thing in common. They had what it took to solve problems. Tall tales are full of problems and contests. The hero may be trying to tame the fiercest bear, stop a cyclone from coming, outthink the quickest thinker, or beat the latest machine. Whatever the problem, the hero solves it because of his or her daring, skill, or strength.

Fill in the story map below for a tall tale you will write. First, list a problem that your folk hero will face. Then exaggerate the steps he or she will take to solve the problem. Also, list the setting (where and when the story takes place) and the characters. Remember: Your hero will have traits that are larger than life. Later, use at least two of these words to write your tall tale.

description	enjoy	exaggeration	fact	fiction
greatest	hero	imagination	independent	invent
irregular	spectacular	successful	transform	

Story Map

Setting: _____

Hero: _____

Traits: _____ _____ _____

Other Characters: _____ _____

Problem: _____

    Step 1: _____

    Step 2: _____

    Step 3: _____

Solution: _____

Writer's Tip

Mix fact with imagination and exaggeration to write your tall tale.

Writer's Challenge

Now use your story map to write your tall tale. Use vivid words to describe your hero, and "speak" in a humorous voice. State your problem and solution clearly, but exaggerate the details. Use two or more of the words from the box above.

Statue of Paul Bunyan and Babe the Blue Ox

Name _____

> ## Helpful Hints

A **suffix** is a word part added to the end of a **base word** or **root**. Suffixes change the meaning of words or make new words.

wish + **ful** = wish**ful**   pain + **less** = pain**less**   bold + **ness** = bold**ness**

Add the **suffix er** to compare *two* things.   bright + **er** = bright**er**

Add the **suffix est** to compare *more than two* things   dark + **est** = dark**est**

Wheeler Peak

⭐ **Read each sentence. Draw one line under the word that compares two things. Draw two lines under the word that compares more than two things.**

1. The highest peak in New Mexico is Wheeler Peak.

2. At 13,361 feet, Wheeler Peak is 718 feet higher than Arizona's Humphreys Peak.

3. The tallest building in Oklahoma City, the Liberty Tower, has 36 stories.

4. The Liberty Tower is shorter than a bank in Tulsa.

5. The population of Arizona is greater than that of New Mexico.

6. Oklahoma has the smallest area of the four Southwestern states.

7. Texas is the largest Southwestern state of all.

8. Arizona is the newest state in the Southwest; it joined the Union in 1912, about a month after New Mexico did.

9. Texas is the oldest Southwestern state. It joined the Union late in 1845.

10. Texas is an older state than Oklahoma is.

11. The fastest way to get from Albuquerque to Phoenix is to go south through national forest land.

WORK TOGETHER

Form a small group. Use an atlas, an almanac, an encyclopedia, or the Internet to find out about these Southwestern states: Arizona, New Mexico, Oklahoma, and Texas. Compare facts by using the suffixes **er** and **est**.

Helpful Hints

Sometimes, you need to make spelling changes before adding **er** or **est**.

Double the final consonant of a one-syllable, short-vowel word before adding **er** or **est**.

re**d** + **er** = re**dd**er   ho**t** + **est** = ho**tt**est

Change **y** to **i** before adding **er** or **est**.

tin**y** + **er** = tin**i**er   sturd**y** + **est** = sturd**i**est

Drop **silent** e before adding **er** or **est**.

wid**e** + **er** = wid**e**r   fin**e** + **est** = fin**e**st

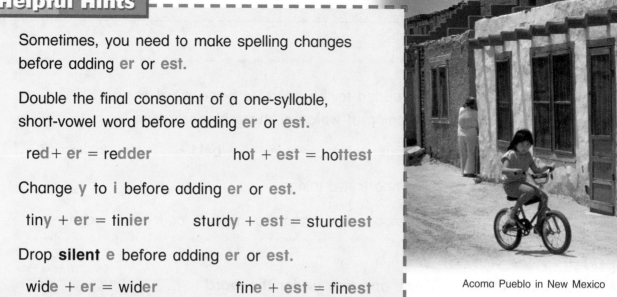

Acoma Pueblo in New Mexico

⭐ **Add er and est to each base word. Write the new words in the chart.**

Base Word	Base Word + *er*	Base Word + *est*
1. nice		
2. sad		
3. friendly		

⭐ **Add er or est to the base word in the box below to complete each sentence correctly.**

grand	keen	old	safe

4. The Acoma Pueblo in New Mexico is the _____ continuously lived-in city in the United States.

5. In 1540, Francisco Coronado wrote that the pueblo's location on a huge mesa made it one of the _____ cities he had ever seen.

6. John Wesley Powell wrote that the Grand Canyon was indeed the _____ place of all.

7. Powell had a _____ knowledge of geology than the explorer, Zebulon Pike.

Home Involvement Activity What is the **high**est peak, **tall**est building, **old**est town, **deep**est lake, **larg**est city, and so on, in your state? Find out together. Record the information on a fact sheet or chart.

Name _____

The **suffix** ful means "full of."   The **suffix** less means "without."

powerful = full of power   painless = without pain

The **suffix** ish means "like," "somewhat," or "belonging to a nation or people."

childish behavior   yellowish light   Spanish dances

If a word ends in **silent** e, drop the e before adding ish.

a whitish color   a bluish sky

The **suffix** like means "resembling."

a lifelike statue   a dreamlike experience

Cinco de Mayo dancers

⭐ **Combine a base word with a suffix in the box to form a new word. Then use the new word in a phrase or sentence that shows its meaning. Write the words and the sentences on the lines.**

Base Words

| baby | beauty | business | desert |
| thought | skill | Swede | worth |

Suffixes

| ful | ish | like | less |
---

1. _____ _____

2. _____ _____

3. _____ _____

4. _____ _____

5. _____ _____

6. _____ _____

7. _____ _____

8. _____ _____

CHALLENGE ◀

The suffixes ful and less are opposite in meaning.

careful/careless

Make a list of opposite words that use the suffixes ful and less.

Helpful Hints

The **suffix y** means "full of," "tending to," or "like."

salty   sticky   watery

When a word ends in **silent e,** usually drop the **e** before adding **y.**

juic**e** + **y** = juic**y**   nois**e** + **y** = nois**y**

When a word ends in a single consonant after a short vowel, double the consonant before adding **y.**

fu**n** + **y** = fu**nny**   dri**p** + **y** = dri**ppy**

The **suffix ly** means "in a certain way."

Quick**ly** means "in a quick way."

When you add **ly** to a word that ends in **le,** drop the **le.**

bubb**le** + **ly** = bubb**ly**   crumb**le** + **ly** = crumb**ly**

When a word ends in **y,** change the **y** to an **i** before adding **ly.**

eas**y** + **ly** = eas**ily**   merr**y** + **ly** = merr**ily**

On the line, add y or ly to the word in bold type.

1. full of **storms**   _____

2. in a **humble** way   _____

3. in a **careless** way   _____

4. full of **dirt**   _____

5. full of or like **ice**   _____

6. in a **happy** way   _____

7. like a **wave**   _____

8. tending to **cling**   _____

9. in a **terrible** way   _____

10. full of **clouds**   _____

11. in a **warm** way   _____

Stormy sky over Saguaro National Monument

LESSON 60: Suffixes
-y, -ly, -ish, -like, -ful, -less

Home Involvement Activity Write each suffix from this lesson on an index card. Shuffle the cards. For each card you pick, build a word. Then use the word in a sentence about the weather.

Name _____

The **suffix** ship means "state or condition of," "office of," or "skill."

Partnership is the state of being partners.

The **suffix** ness means "state or quality of."

Blindness is the state of being blind.

The **suffix** hood means "state, quality, or condition of."

Childhood is the time or state of being a child.

The **suffix** ment means "act or result of" or "state of being."

Disappointment is the state of being disappointed.

The **suffix** some means "like or tending to."

Troublesome means tending to cause trouble.

⭐ **Join each base word and suffix.**
Write the new word on the line.

1. citizen + ship _____
2. adult + hood _____
3. nervous + ness _____
4. measure + ment _____
5. burden + some _____
6. penman + ship _____
7. improve + ment _____
8. neighbor + hood _____
9. awe + some _____
10. bright + ness _____
11. friend + ship _____

Citizenship ceremony

CHALLENGE

The suffix some can also describe a grouping, such as a **three**some. Write a sentence about sports using **two**some and **four**some.

Read each phrase. Underline the suffix ship, ness, hood, ment, or some in each word in bold type.

1. his **boyhood** in Arizona
2. won the **championship**
3. new to **parenthood**
4. a worn **pavement**
5. has **leadership** qualities
6. a new **development**
7. takes **ownership**
8. a **quarrelsome** couple
9. graceful **movement**
10. pleasure and **happiness**
11. heated **arguments**

12. the **seriousness** of the problem
13. **tiresome** chores
14. felt deep **sadness**
15. a **fearsome** storm

Galveston Harbor after hurricane

Complete each sentence below. Choose from the words in bold type above.

16. A _____ hurricane battered the Gulf Coast of Texas.

17. Almost at once, the _____ began to buckle under our feet.

18. _____ neighbors argued over how to protect boats and homes.

19. The mayor and the police chief showed strong _____ qualities during the crisis.

20. Quick action or _____ was needed to rescue the victims.

21. The community felt great _____ for the town's loss.

22. Everyone was aware of the _____ of the damage.

23. Cleaning up would be a long and _____ process.

24. _____ arose over how to begin the cleanup.

25. We all felt _____ when the town was restored.

126

LESSON 61: Suffixes
-ship, -ness, -hood, -ment, -some

Home Involvement Activity Discuss the feelings of **enjoy**ment, **amaze**ment, and **resent**ment. Talk with family members about situations and events that evoke these feelings.

Name _____

Helpful Hints

The **suffix ity** means "state or condition."

real + **ity** = real**ity**

The **suffix ive** means "relating to" or "tending to."

protect + **ive** = protect**ive**

When words end in **silent e**, drop the **e** before adding the suffixes **ity** or **ive**.

sincere + **ity** = sincer**ity**   create + **ive** = creat**ive**

The **suffix age** means "act, condition, or result of" or "collection of."

break**age**   bagg**age**

The **suffix age** may also mean "cost of," "home of," or "amount of."

post**age**   orphan**age**   short**age**

When a word ends in **y** after a consonant, change the **y** to **i** before adding **age**.

carry + **age** = carr**iage**

When a **suffix** that begins with a vowel follows a one-syllable, short-vowel word ending in a consonant, double the consonant before adding the suffix.

lug + **age** = lu**ggage**

⭐ **Underline the suffix in each word in bold type.**

1. picked up the **baggage**

2. put the box in **storage**

3. an **active** volcano

4. the ship's **wreckage**

5. sends a **package**

6. a **destructive** storm

7. **supportive** friends

8. a week of high **humidity**

9. too much **publicity**

10. a happy **marriage**

11. car with low **mileage**

12. **possibility** of rain

CHALLENGE

Unscramble the word in bold type. Underline its suffix. Then write your own sentence for the unscrambled word.

*Mom is an **xtuevicee** at the bank.*

The **suffix** ion, sion, or tion means "act or result of."

reflect**ion**   confu**sion**   crea**tion**

Sometimes, when a word ends in **silent e**, drop the **e** before adding **ion**.

tense → ten**sion**   rotate → rota**tion**

The spelling of a word may change when the suffix ion, sion, or tion is added.

decide = deci**sion**   **divide** = divi**sion**

persuade = persua**sion**   **describe** = descri**ption**

Read about the Grand Canyon. Add the suffix ion to the word in the word box that best completes each sentence. Make any needed spelling changes. Write the new word on the line.

confuse	create	direct	elevate	protect

Many people are fascinated by the Grand Canyon. We can all agree that it is

big and beautiful. Yet there is some **(1)** _____ about its age. We do know
that 65 million years ago, the rim was at sea level. Somewhere between 5 million and

20 million years ago, the Colorado River took its present **(2)** _____.

Its flow caused the **(3)** _____ of the canyon. As the river began to carve

out the canyon, the **(4)** _____ of the land changed. It began to rise.
Today, the South Rim is 7,500 feet above sea level in places. The North Rim is
1,000 feet higher. Nature's masterpiece of the American Southwest deserves our

care and **(5)** _____.

A view from the North Rim of the Grand Canyon

LESSON 62: Suffixes
-ity, -ive, -age, -ion/-sion/-tion

Home Involvement Activity What is the most magnificent natural site you have seen together? Talk about it. Use as many words with the suffix ion, sion, or tion as you can.

Name _____

Helpful Hints

The **suffix** able or ible means "able to" or "capable of."

An **enjoy**able movie is capable of giving enjoyment.
A **sens**ible person is capable of showing good sense.

The **suffix** ance or ence means "act of" or "state of being."

Avoidance is the act of avoiding.
Difference is the state of being different.

There is no rule for whether to use able or ible, or ance or ence. It is best to check a dictionary when you are unsure about which spelling is correct.

Read each statement. Add the suffix in parentheses to the word in bold type to form a word that will complete the sentence. Write the word on the line.

WORD STRATEGY

If a base word ends in **silent** e, you drop the e before adding able or ible. Add able to these words:

believe   inflate

Notice some exceptions to the rule:

lovable *or* loveable
manageable
knowledgeable

1. (able) If you can **break** this vase, then it must be

   _____.

2. (ible) If you can **digest** certain foods, then they must be

   _____.

3. (able) If you can **manage** your pets, then they are

   _____.

4. (ible) If you can **flex** a drinking straw, then it must be

   _____.

5. (ance) If something **annoys** you, then it is an _____.

6. (ence) If you **persist** until you finish a task, then you have

   _____.

7. (ence) If you are **intelligent,** then you have _____.

8. (ence) If you are **confident,** then you have _____.

★ **Use each of the words in the box in a sentence that shows its meaning.**

| independence | predictable | appearance |

1. _____

_____

2. _____

_____

3. _____

_____

★ **Fill in the circle of the word that completes each sentence correctly. Then write the word on the line.**

4. I can never get _____ sitting on a wooden bench.
   ○ comfortable   ○ washable   ○ legible

5. Getting to know people of different cultures helps us develop _____.
   ○ appearance   ○ tolerance   ○ brilliance

6. His _____ from school on Tuesday made him miss the test.
   ○ independence   ○ absence   ○ avoidance

7. Bridget was thrilled to get a letter of _____ to college.
   ○ acceptance   ○ existence   ○ dependence

8. Last year, I won my school's gold medal for _____ in science.
   ○ excellence   ○ difference   ○ confidence

9. Granddad drove a _____ in the 1950s.
   ○ perishable   ○ deductible   ○ convertible

130

LESSON 63: Suffixes
-able/-ible, and **-ance/-ence**

Home Involvement Activity Ordinary objects are
measurable in many ways. For example, you can
measure a jar by its height, weight, or capacity.
Choose objects. List the ways they are **measur**able.

Name _____

> ## Helpful Hints

Some words have *more than one* **prefix.**

The word **rediscover** adds the **prefixes re** and **dis** to **cover.**
The word **disentangle** adds the **prefixes dis** and **en** to **tangle.**

Some words have *more than one* **suffix.**

Creatively adds the **suffixes ive** and **ly** to the base word **create.**
Forgetfulness adds the **suffixes ful** and **ness** to the word **forget.**

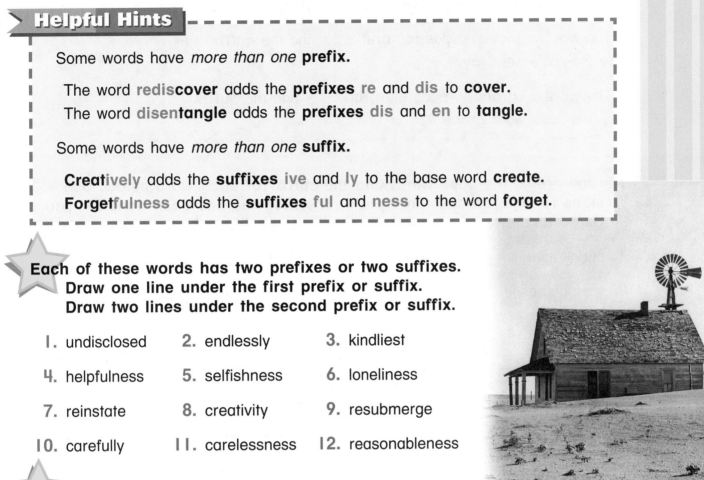

★ **Each of these words has two prefixes or two suffixes.
Draw one line under the first prefix or suffix.
Draw two lines under the second prefix or suffix.**

1. undisclosed
2. endlessly
3. kindliest
4. helpfulness
5. selfishness
6. loneliness
7. reinstate
8. creativity
9. resubmerge
10. carefully
11. carelessness
12. reasonableness

★ **Read these sentences about Oklahoma. Underline the
word in each sentence that has *more than one
suffix.* Then circle each suffix in the word.
Write the base word on the line.**

Abandoned farmhouse in
the Dust Bowl

13. In the 1930s, dust storms fearlessly
swept through Oklahoma and ruined
the land. _____

14. Oklahoma-born songwriter Woody
Guthrie actively worked to expose
the hard lives of farmers during
the 1930s. _____

15. Guthrie told of the powerlessness
of poor farmers who had been
hurt by the dust storms. _____

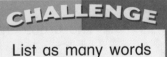

List as many words
as you can with
more than one
prefix or suffix that
can complete the
following sentence:

*Her _____
made her the right
choice for mayor.*

Helpful Hint

Some words have both a **prefix** *and* a **suffix**.

The word **en**joy**able** adds the **prefix en** and the **suffix able** to the base word **joy.**

The word **dis**grace**ful** adds the **prefix dis** and the **suffix ful** to the base word **grace.**

★ **Write the prefix, the base word, and the suffix for each word below. Use + signs to separate the three parts. The first one has been done for you. Use a dictionary, if needed, to check the spelling of any base words.**

1. enrichment   _en + rich + ment_

2. disappearance _____

3. illegally _____

4. coauthorship _____

5. replacement _____

6. immaturity _____

7. unbelievable _____

8. incompletion _____

★ **Fill in the circle of the word that completes each sentence. Then write the word on the line.**

9. _____ arose at the meeting.
   - ○ Replacements   ○ Unreasonable   ○ Disagreements

10. The arguments were about who would buy the _____.
    - ○ refreshments   ○ distrustful   ○ independence

11. We refused to tip the _____ waiter.
    - ○ unchangeable   ○ cooperative   ○ unfriendly

12. For $1.49, you can get _____ cups of soda at the all-night market.
    - ○ exchangeable   ○ refillable   ○ unselfish

Home Involvement Activity Choose one of the base words from this page, such as **place.** Have a contest to see who can add the most prefixes and suffixes to this base word to build new words.

Name _____

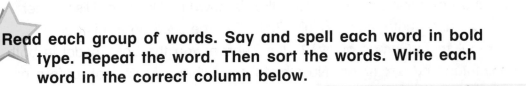

⭐ **Read each group of words. Say and spell each word in bold type. Repeat the word. Then sort the words. Write each word in the correct column below.**

- an **active** child

- too much **publicity**

- a **thoughtful** gift

- gave a **sensible** answer

- showed poor **judgment**

- spoke with **confidence**

- **friendliest** student of all

- a **believable** story

- making tough **decisions**

- with all **seriousness**

Statue in Oklahoma of a pioneer woman and her son

- a **troublesome** situation

- won the **championship**

- a **subscription** to a magazine

- a **lifelike** statue

- responsibility of **parenthood**

- long and happy **marriage**

- an **unselfish** person

- **importance** to the community

Words That Start with A – H	Words That Start with I – P	Words That Start with Q – Z

Jim Thorpe was born in 1887. He was one of a pair of twin boys born into the Sac and Fox Indian tribes on land that is now in Oklahoma. His mother gave him a name that means "Bright Path." Thorpe lived up to his name.

At the Olympic Games of 1912, Jim Thorpe won the gold medal in both the pentathlon and decathlon. No athlete has achieved this feat, before or since. The King of Sweden, who presented Thorpe with his medals, called him "the greatest athlete in the world."

Choose a famous athlete—past or present. Do some research. Write a sports column about the person for your school or local newspaper. Give highlights from your athlete's life and career. Use at least two of these spelling words.

active	publicity	thoughtful	sensible	judgment
confidence	friendliest	believable		decisions
seriousness	troublesome	championship		subscription
lifelike	parenthood	marriage	unselfish	importance

_____

_____

_____

_____

_____

_____

_____

_____

Writer's Tip

Answer the 5*Ws* in your column. Your readers need to know *who* your story is about, *what* happened, *when* and *where* it took place, and *why* or *how* it happened.

Jim Thorpe at 1912 Olympics

Writer's Challenge

Jim Thorpe had great athletic ability in football, track, baseball, boxing, hockey, lacrosse, archery, tennis, and swimming. In a paragraph, explain why someone might be good at so many sports.

Name _____

Take an imaginary hike through Big Bend National Park in America's Southwest and experience the park's unusual plants and animals. Then answer the questions that follow.

Deep in the Heart of...Big Bend

by Bud McDonald

Big Bend National Park

To find Big Bend on a map, look at the southwestern portion of Texas, the part of the state that juts out beneath New Mexico. You'll notice that it also lies along the border that divides the United States from Mexico. Big Bend gets its name from the giant U-turn made by the Rio Grande that forms the southern boundary of this national park.

Many prickly desert plants and stinging, biting desert animals make their home at Big Bend. Thirty kinds of snakes live here, including five species of rattlesnakes. Tarantulas and scorpions make their home in this arid land, as well. Herds of deer add their graceful beauty. *Javelina* (a small, native wild pig), roadrunners, and armadillos thrive. Coyotes and mountain lions live here, too.

More than 400 species of birds live at Big Bend or pass through it during the year. That's more birds than are found in any other national park in the United States. There are species of plants at Big Bend that live nowhere else.

One reason for the great variety of life is because Big Bend has many different habitats: deserts, mountains, wooded river bottoms, desert springs, and canyons.

Visitors to Big Bend will see Native American cliff paintings thousands of years old. These ancient pictures help us to imagine the way life was at Big Bend.

Reader's Response

1. **Why is Big Bend home to so many different kinds of wildlife?**

2. **Visitors to Big Bend can see ancient cliff paintings. Why do you think people painted these pictures?**

3. **Imagine that it is thousands of years ago. You are living at Big Bend. What is your life like? Why?**

Big Bend's interesting geography—its deserts, mountains, and river canyons—its unusual plants and animals, its ancient cliff paintings, and miles of hiking trails make it an ideal place for people to visit. In fact, its haunting sights and sounds, as well as its lush smells provide the perfect setting for an adventure.

Now choose a place that would make an interesting topic for a travel article. Your place could be a park, a city or village, or your hometown. Include facts about the geography of the area and a brief history. Describe two interesting places to visit. Include a small map, a photograph, or an illustration. Use at least two of these words.

traveling protective features photograph description activity
recreation geography respectful unfamiliar transportation beautiful

Armadillo

_____

_____

_____

_____

_____

_____

_____

_____

_____

_____

Writer's Tip

Choose the most interesting information that will make your audience want to experience the place for themselves.

Javelina, or peccary

Writer's Challenge

Turn your travel article into a travel brochure. Add a list of interesting places to visit and activities for the whole family to enjoy. You might include information about where to eat, sleep, and shop. Use vivid words that will support your descriptions and details.

Name _____

★ **Look** at the word-part chart below. You can use it to form many words. For example, you can form the word contraction by combining CI + B2 + H3.

	1	2	3
A	un	create	ment
B	trans	tract	ible
C	con	term	ly
D	ex	form	tion
E	re	ject	less
F	dis	sense	ful
G	de	gage	ness
H	in	turn	ion
I	en	circle	ive
J	semi	script	ity

Century plant at Big Bend National Park

★ **Use** the word-part chart to decode these words. On the lines, write the words that you get from these letters and numbers. Make spelling changes as needed.

1. BI + D2 _____

2. II + I2 _____

3. JI + I2 _____

4. F2 + B3 _____

5. B2 + H3 _____

6. D2 + E3 + G3 _____

7. FI + B2 + H3 _____

8. HI + E2 + H3 _____

9. DI + B2 + H3 _____

10. II + G2 + A3 _____

★ **Use** the word-part chart to encode these words. Write the letters and the numbers on the lines.

11. reject _____

12. creativity _____

Read the passage. For each numbered blank, there is a choice of words below. Circle the letter of the word that completes the sentence correctly.

The Sonoran Desert of Arizona is a land of dry plains and mountains. It hosts a variety of cacti, shrubs, and small trees. It is home to the prickly pear, *cholla,* and barrel cactus. *Palo verde,* ironwood, and mesquite trees grow here. Many desert animals dwell here, too. These hardy creatures know how to live **1** in this harsh place.

Perhaps the best known **2** of the Sonoran Desert is a special type of cactus. The stately saguaro [suh-(G)WAHR-oh] cactus grows here and in northern Mexico only. Unlike trees, the saguaro has no leaves. Its shape helps it to hold water and to **3** water loss. The saguaro loses less than a glass of water a day. (Ordinary trees can lose hundreds of gallons in one day.) Naturally, the saguaro stores water for the desert's long dry spells. It also provides food and shelter for desert animals.

1. **a.** successfully   **b.** forgetfully   **c.** helplessly

2. **a.** infection   **b.** inspector   **c.** inhabitant

3. **a.** deduce   **b.** produce   **c.** reduce

Saguaro Cacti in the Sonoran Desert

Reread the passage to answer the questions. Circle the letter of the answer.

4. What is true about the saguaro?
   a. It grows in snowy mountains.
   b. It has bushy leaves.
   c. It holds great amounts of water.
   d. It scares away animals.

5. What is a *cholla?*
   a. a kind of home
   b. a kind of fruit
   c. a kind of animal
   d. a kind of cactus

Extend & Apply

Write a glossary entry for the saguaro. Include its pronunciation, definition, an original sentence, and a picture. Use one word with a prefix and a suffix.

Picture This

Anyone who has ever lived in or visited the West is familiar with its natural beauty. In this unit, you will meet a photographer and many other people who fell in love with this region.

The photographer Ansel Adams first visited Yosemite National Park on a family vacation. It was 1916, and he was fourteen years old. For Adams, it was love at first sight. He took his first pictures of Yosemite on that trip. He would go back there again and again.

Ansel Adams was a fine photographer. In 1941, officials of the United States government asked Adams to go to national parks in the West. They hoped he would photograph wild natural areas for a set of murals. Adams gladly took the job. He wanted Americans to share in the beauty of their country.

The Mural Project lasted for less than a year. The reason: The United States had entered World War II. Fortunately, in that short time, Adams had turned out more than 250 photographs of the West.

Adams' wilderness photos set the tone for the kind of work he would do for the rest of his career. He also worked to protect nature. In fact, his photos inspired artists and conservationists alike. His magnificent pictures opened all our eyes to the beauty of the American land.

Critical Thinking

1. **What did the U.S. government want Ansel Adams to do? Why?**

2. **Do you think that photographers and artists can influence the way people see the world? Explain.**

3. **If you could step into Ansel Adams' photograph of the Grand Tetons at the top of the page, how would you feel?**

Picture This

Anyone who has ever lived in or visited the West is familiar with its natural beauty. In this unit, you will meet a photographer and many other people who fell in love with this region.

The photographer Ansel Adams first visited Yosemite National Park on a family vacation. It was 1916, and he was fourteen years old. For Adams, it was love at first sight. He took his first pictures of Yosemite on that trip. He would go back there again and again.

Ansel Adams was a fine photographer. In 1941, officials of the United States government asked Adams to go to national parks in the West. They hoped he would photograph wild natural areas for a set of murals. Adams gladly took the job. He wanted Americans to share in the beauty of their country.

The Mural Project lasted for less than a year. The reason: The United States had entered World War II. Fortunately, in that short time, Adams had turned out more than 250 photographs of the West.

Adams' wilderness photos set the tone for the kind of work he would do for the rest of his career. He also worked to protect nature. In fact, his photos inspired artists and conservationists alike. His magnificent pictures opened all our eyes to the beauty of the American land.

Critical Thinking

1. What did the U.S. government want Ansel Adams to do? Why?
2. Do you think that photographers and artists can influence the way people see the world? Explain.
3. If you could step into Ansel Adams' photograph of the Grand Tetons at the top of the page, how would you feel?

LESSON 68: Introduction to Context Clues   139

Dear Family,

In Unit 5, your child will learn about the importance of using context clues as a word-study strategy. By using context clues, your child will discover the meaning of unfamiliar words and will become a better reader. The theme of this unit is the *West,* including its people and history.

Context clues can help a reader figure out the meaning of an unfamiliar word. By understanding the context (the nearby words in a sentence or paragraph), your child will be able to unlock the meaning of a word.

Family Focus

• Read together the nonfiction selection on page 139. Look at Adams' wilderness photograph of Grand Teton National Park in Wyoming. Discuss the subject and the composition of the photo. How does the photo make each member of your family feel?

• Together, look at a map of the United States. Identify the states that make up the West: California, Nevada, Montana, Utah, Colorado, Idaho, and Wyoming. Which of these states have you or friends visited? Which would you like to visit? Plan a real or an imagined road trip through the West.

LINKS TO LEARNING

To extend learning together, you might explore:

Web Sites
www.adamsgallery.com
www.nps.gov

Videos
America's Historic Trails, PBS Home Video, 6 videos.

Our National Parks, PBS Home Video.

The West, a film by Ken Burns and Stephen Ives, PBS Home Video, 9 videos.

Literature
Ansel Adams: The National Park Service Photographs, ©1995.

Justin and the Best Biscuits in the World by Mildred Pitts Walter, ©1986.

Name _____

You can use **context clues** to figure out the meaning of an unknown word and to develop a better understanding of what you are reading. By using context clues and your own **experience,** you usually can get the general meaning of a word. Look for context clues *before* or *after* an unfamiliar word to help you unlock meaning that may not be stated directly.

California sunset

Read each sentence. Then underline the best answer to the question. On the line, explain your thinking. Use your experience. Look for context clues to help you understand each sentence.

1. The setting sun turns the sky a glorious shade of purple and gold.
   What time of day is it?   morning   noon   early evening

   What context clue(s) helped you? _____

2. When the alarm sounded, the class quickly filed outside and waited for news.
   What was going on?   wake-up call   fire drill   lunchtime

   What context clue(s) helped you? _____

3. The group knew that empty canteens would mean serious problems.
   Where might the group be?   in a desert   by a stream   at a movie

   What context clue(s) helped you? _____

4. We were out of granola, so we prepared some oatmeal.
   What was going on?
      grocery shopping   packing lunch   making breakfast

   What context clue(s) helped you? _____

5. It's lucky that we had on our life jackets when we capsized and that the shore was not far.
   What was going on?
      a boat tipped over   a plane landed   swimmers raced

   What context clue(s) helped you? _____

CHALLENGE

Use your experience to explain to a friend the scene being described in this sentence:

   It was bleak outside, but I didn't need to open my umbrella.

You can use your experience, along with context clues, to figure out a missing word in a sentence. Read carefully. Think about the meaning of the sentence. Here's an example:

I have two _____ cats and three female ones.

Think about what you know. The word **male** makes sense in this sentence.

⭐ **Complete each sentence with a word from the box below. Look for context clues to determine the missing word. Write the word on the line. Make sure it makes sense in the sentence.**

dull	floss	jacket	pudding	light

1. I stirred the _____ constantly so that it wouldn't stick to the pot.

2. This knife is too _____ for slicing a whole watermelon.

3. Traffic came to a complete halt when the _____ changed.

4. I always brush my teeth, but I don't always _____ them.

5. The _____ didn't fit comfortably, so I tried on the next size.

⭐ **Each sentence below is missing a word. Look for context clues to help you figure out what the word should be. Then on the line, write a word that makes sense in the sentence. There may be more than one choice.**

6. I can't _____ whether to order a taco or a burrito.

7. When you take the pie out of the oven, be sure to use _____.

8. It's smart to _____ your plants before you go away for the weekend.

9. Control the _____ on the stereo so that you don't disturb the neighbors.

10. The four _____ on the car are worn out, so I'll have to replace them.

11. As you climb high up the mountain, the _____ feels thinner and cooler.

12. In circus class, I'm learning how to _____ a plate on the end of a broomstick.

LESSON 69: Context Clues—
Experience

Home Involvement Activity Find a number of interesting sentences in a newspaper. Take turns reading each sentence aloud, but leave out one word. Challenge your family to suggest a word that makes sense.

Name _____

> **Helpful Hint**

Sometimes, you may not know the meaning of a word in a sentence. Try using **context clues** to help you figure out the definition of the word. One way to do this is by looking for other words in the sentence that may give a **definition.** This definition may differ from what you would find in a dictionary. Yet it can help you unlock the meaning of the unfamiliar word.

★ **Read the sentences. Underline the word or words that give a definition of the word in bold type.**

1. Bison live on the National Bison Range in Moiese, Montana. This range gives the wild animals a **refuge,** a safe place where they can live free of danger.

2. **Drought,** a long period of dry weather, is always a danger in Western states.

3. A **jackelope** is an imaginary animal that seems to be a cross between a jackrabbit and an antelope.

4. Miners came to the West to search for gold, silver, and copper. **Entrepreneurs,** people who took business risks in order to make profits, soon followed.

Bison on National Bison Range in Montana

5. Astronauts wanted a place to practice moon landings. They found it in the bowl-shaped holes of **craters** in a national monument in Idaho.

6. Montana's rocky **bluffs**—high, steep cliffs—are one feature of the state's interesting landforms.

7. In a **depleted** mine, few minerals are left to dig out.

8. Trout fishers need to lure their trout to bite. Therefore, they cast colorful flies to **entice,** or attract, the hungry fish.

9. Dad collects mining **relics,** displaying some of the precious old objects in his office.

WORK TOGETHER

Think of a word that you think a partner will not know. Use it in a sentence in which other words define it. Have your partner use the context clues in the sentence to figure out the meaning of the word.

Many words may have more than one meaning. The particular meaning depends on the **context** in which the word appears. For example, you know that a **drum** is a musical instrument. However, a **drum** is also a metal barrel used to hold oil or other liquids.

Study the diagram of the handsaw below. Use the diagram to figure out the meaning of the following words or labels. On the lines below, write a sentence for each word as it relates to the handsaw. Be sure that other words in the sentence define the word.

back

blade

toe

teeth

handle

heel

1. toe _____

_____

2. back _____

_____

3. blade _____

_____

4. handle _____

_____

5. heel _____

_____

6. teeth _____

_____

Home Involvement Activity Select a household appliance or a piece of furniture. Choose a word that identifies a part of the item. Use it in a sentence that defines the specific meaning of the word.

Name _____

Helpful Hint

You know that a word may be defined within the **context** of a sentence. Sometimes, that definition looks formal. Other times, it gives meaning through example.

Max is the most **mercurial** person I know; one minute he's happy, the next moment he's sad.

Max's mood changes often. His mood is not constant. This is what **mercurial** means in this sentence.

Daguerreotype of gold miners in California, 1850

Read the sentences. Underline the word or words that define the word in bold type. Use the context of the sentence to figure out the meaning of the word.

1. Gold miners often had **daguerreotypes** taken of themselves; this was before modern photography improved upon what early cameras could do.

2. Levi Strauss was a **shrewd** peddler. He knew that the forty-niners needed sturdy pants; he made a fortune by cleverly inventing and selling blue jeans to miners.

3. Gold miners never welcomed **intruders.** The miners did not want uninvited guests snooping around their claims.

4. We knew that the two miners were in **cahoots;** they were always whispering secrets to each other.

5. In the 1850s, a large number of **emigrants** left Europe. These people left their countries to make a new life in the West.

6. They hiked to the top of the largest **butte** in the valley; like the other mounds, it was freestanding and flat on top.

7. One of the diggers at the site was a **curmudgeon;** he was always in a bad mood and ready with a rude remark.

CHALLENGE

Write one sentence each for three of the words above. Be sure that each sentence shows the meaning of the word.

The sentences below tell about Mesa Verde National Park in Colorado and the Anasazi who moved there about 1,500 years ago. Read each sentence. Figure out the meaning of the word in bold type. Then on the lines, write your own definition of the word.

Mesa Verde National Park in Colorado

1. The Anasazi used to be a **nomadic** people, moving from place to place in search of food and a new home. By the time they got to Mesa Verde, they had settled into farming.

   _____

   _____

2. The Anasazi built small villages on the top of **mesas;** these hills were smaller than plateaus but also flat on top.

   _____

   _____

3. These people lived in multiroom pit houses. The Anasazi also built **kivas**—round rooms which were partly underground and were used for religious ceremonies.

   _____

   _____

4. They built sturdy houses from **adobe** bricks; these bricks were made of sun-dried clay, which kept the inside of the house comfortable in heat or cold.

   _____

   _____

5. The population of Mesa Verde grew. By A.D. 1000, the Anasazi began to use **masonry** to build large stone houses.

   _____

   _____

LESSON 71: Context Clues—
Definitions 2

Home Involvement Activity Discuss the different rooms in a house and their uses. Cut out or draw pictures of these rooms and label each one.

Name _____

> **Helpful Hint**

Another way to use **context clues** is to look for a list, or **series.** You can often figure out what a word means by thinking about the other words in the same series.

When our garden blooms, I love to see the purple tulips, irises, and **hyacinths.**

You may not know the word **hyacinths,** but you know they bloom in a garden. Your experience should help you realize that **hyacinths** are flowers.

Craters of the Moon National Monument in Idaho

Read each sentence. Underline the series of words that belong together in the sentence. Then fill in the circle of the choice that tells how the words in the series are linked.

1. Craters of the Moon National Monument in Idaho is a great place to visit. There you can see scoria, obsidian, pumice, lava bombs, and other volcanic stone.

   This is a series of _____.
   ○ bullets   ○ rocks   ○ diamonds

2. Idaho's most famous food crop includes bakers, mashers, russets, and plain old spuds.

   This is a series of _____.
   ○ flowers   ○ cattle   ○ potatoes

3. The visitors' center has information about the sage grouse, quail, pheasant, and partridge in the area.

   This is a series of _____.
   ○ game birds   ○ fish   ○ insects

4. If you bring the tempera, the oils, and the watercolors, I'll bring the paper and frames.

   This is a series of _____.
   ○ snack foods   ○ art supplies   ○ fabrics

> **WORD STRATEGY**

You don't always need the exact meaning of a word in order to understand it. A broad meaning may do. Read this sentence:

The menu has New England clam chowder, corn chowder, and **bouillabaisse.**

This French word names a kind of _____.

⭐ **Look for words in a series. Use these words and other context clues to write a simple meaning for each word in bold type.**

1. The cowhands taught us how to tie square knots, **bowlines,** half hitches, and slipknots.

   _____

   _____

2. Horses can be trained to walk, pace, trot, **canter,** and gallop to certain commands.

   _____

3. You may substitute **filberts,** pecans, almonds, or cashews for walnuts in this recipe.

   _____

4. The butternut, **crookneck,** white bush, and acorn are all members of the squash family.

   _____

5. You can walk, stroll, or **shamble**—just arrive at soccer practice on time!

   _____

6. I can't tell a sailboat from a canoe or a **schooner,** but I'd love to ride in one.

   _____

7. Is there a grocery, supermarket, or **bodega** around the corner?

   _____

8. That specialty shop sells bowlers, Stetsons, berets, and **turbans.**

   _____

9. We packed the first-aid kit with bandages, tape, cotton, soap, and a **salve.**

   _____

LESSON 72: Context Clues—
Words in a Series I

Home Involvement Activity Play a listing game. Choose a category, such as animals, vegetables, cities, or athletes. In turn, name something in that category that begins with a, then b, then c, and so on.

Name _____

> ## Helpful Hint
>
> Remember that words in the same **series** as that of an unknown word may give you the **context clues** you need to figure out the meaning of the word.

Star garnet—Idaho's gemstone

★ **Read each short passage about Idaho. Then answer the question that follows the passage. Use context clues to help you.**

1. Idaho is nicknamed the Gem State. Rock hounds all over the state have found fine pieces of **beryl,** jade, jasper, opal, and topaz. Idaho's official gemstone is the star garnet. This stone is found only in Idaho and in India.

   What is **beryl?** _____

2. Hagerman Fossil Beds National Monument is a rare spot. It is along the Snake River, across from a high school. This Idaho park is filled with traces of early North American small mammals. Scientists have found fossils of early horses, camels, **peccary,** and beaver. The fossil beds are more than 3.5 million years old.

   What are **peccary?** _____

3. Buhl, Idaho, is the rainbow trout capital of the nation. This small town on the Snake River leads the United States in research into trout and other freshwater fish. Huge farms in the area raise trout, as well as catfish, salmon, and **tilapia.**

   What are **tilapia?** _____

   _____

4. There are many kinds of landforms throughout the West. Some types of tablelands are the mesa, butte, plateau, **hogback,** and cuesta. All are broad regions of higher land that rise from flatter surfaces. Some people think they look like giant tables.

   What is a **hogback?** _____

   _____

> ## CHALLENGE
>
> Use a map and context clues to understand this statement:
>
> The Snake River **demarcates** Idaho's border with Washington.
>
> What is the meaning of **demarcates?**

Helpful Hint

The **context clues** that give meaning to words in a **series** may appear elsewhere in the passage. Read carefully to find the clues you need.

Student poets at the Cowboy Poetry Gathering

Each passage below is missing a word. Use context clues to figure out a word that could fill in the blank correctly. Write a word that makes sense. Then explain your choice on the lines below.

1. Each year in January, Elko, Nevada, hosts the Cowboy Poetry Gathering. The goal of this event is to preserve cowboy culture. Programs include

   songs, artwork, tall tales, and, of course, _____.

   Explain your choice. _____

   _____

2. Reno, Nevada, has a fine planetarium. It offers public shows that open our minds to the wonders of the night sky. Programs vary all year long. Shows

   may focus on stars, meteors, _____, comets, or eclipses, to name a few popular topics.

   Explain your choice. _____

   _____

3. Wide-open spaces lure fans of outdoor activities to the West. Hikers, skiers,

   horseback riders, and _____ come to play in the great outdoors.

   Explain your choice. _____

   _____

4. Many animals are able to thrive in areas where other animals might suffer.

   These include the scorpion, _____, gecko, and rattlesnake. Such animals adapt to the heat of the Nevada desert by hunting at night.

   Explain your choice. _____

   _____

Home Involvement Activity Work together to think of other answers to items 1–4. Use the context clues given. There are many possible choices.

Name _____

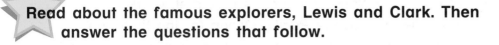

★ **Read about the famous explorers, Lewis and Clark. Then answer the questions that follow.**

Catching Up with Lewis and Clark

from a nonfiction article in Time for Kids magazine

Nobody likes a litterbug, but historians wish that Meriwether Lewis and William Clark had left more behind as they traveled across the North American continent 200 years ago. They cleaned up so well after themselves that it's hard to tell exactly where they stopped on their journey from St. Louis, Missouri, to the Pacific Ocean.

But researchers hope to answer age-old questions about these great <u>trailblazers</u> of the West, whose work made it possible for the U.S. government to claim the Oregon territory. This led to pioneers settling the West in the mid-1800s.

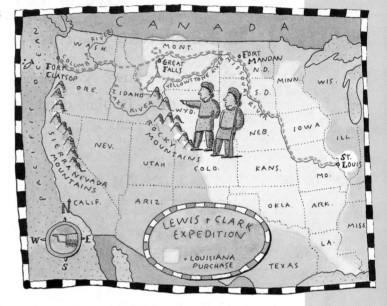

In 1803, President Thomas Jefferson asked Lewis to explore the Louisiana Purchase, a huge area of land that the United States was about to buy from France. He hoped to learn of a water route between the Mississippi River and the Pacific Ocean that would help U.S. trade.

Lewis and his best friend, Clark, left St. Louis in May 1804 with a party of 42 men. They never found the water route, but they became the first U.S. citizens to see many of America's wonders—the endless Great Plains, the Rocky Mountains, and the Pacific. They faced many hardships and dangers, including bear attacks and bitter cold. More than 500 days and 4,000 miles after they had set out, Lewis and Clark reached the Pacific.

The explorers kept superb maps and diaries. They were the first to describe 122 kinds of animals and 178 plants, and to meet many native tribes. But they left barely a trace behind. That makes it hard to say "Lewis and Clark were here!"

📖 Reader's Response

1. Lewis and Clark were **trailblazers**. What context clues helped you figure out the meaning of the word?

2. How did the excellent diaries and maps of Lewis and Clark help the pioneers to settle the West?

3. What experience have you had that can help you identify with the difficult but exciting journey of Lewis and Clark?

Lewis and Clark filled their journals with interesting information. For example, they wrote about Sacajawea, an English-speaking Shoshone woman, who spoke with the Native Americans they met. Clark also described what it felt like to see the Pacific Ocean for the first time. "Ocian in view! O! the joy!" Clark may not have been a good speller, but his diary and Lewis's proved to be the best guidebooks to the West.

Imagine that you are Lewis *and* Clark. Write paired diary entries. Choose an exciting event, such as the day you met Sacajawea, the day a bear attacked, or the day you finally reached the Pacific Ocean. Write two diary entries, one from Lewis's point of view, the other from Clark's. Include at least two of these words.

expedition travel journey explore guide arrived observed sight
magnificent helpful dangerous hardship first next then finally

Lewis

_____

_____

_____

_____

_____

_____

_____

Clark

_____

_____

_____

_____

_____

_____

_____

Writer's Tip

Think about how the two men probably were similar, yet different. This will help you present each explorer's point of view about the same event.

Speaker's Challenge

Imagine that you are a TV reporter. You are telling the news about a scientist's recent discovery of what may have been one of Lewis and Clark's campsites. Tell about the scientist's "dig" and the items that he or she may have found. Explain how this discovery may prove that Lewis and Clark were there!

The Guide Sacajawea with Lewis & Clark, by N. C. Wyeth, 1940.

LESSON 74: Connecting Reading and Writing Comprehension—Relate Reading to Your Own Experience; Synthesize

Name _____

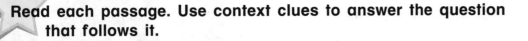

⭐ **Read each passage. Use context clues to answer the question that follows it.**

Migrant workers in Imperial County

1. Imperial County in California has some of the richest farmland in the world. Its main crops are tomatoes, cotton, melons, lettuce, and beets. Yet this area was once a dry and dusty desert. **Irrigation** changed all that. The new canals and sprinkler systems soon gave the region its lush pastures and fields.

   What is **irrigation?** _____

   _____

2. It just wouldn't work—and we were so hot! We turned on two old fans, closed the shades, put on shorts, and drank ice-cold lemonade until the repair person came to fix it.

   What wouldn't work? How do you know? _____

   _____

3. In Spanish, *los gatos* means "the cats." Los Gatos is the name of a small city in California. It was founded in 1868 on part of an old Spanish land grant. Its name **harks back** to past times when mountain lions and wildcats freely roamed the nearby hills.

   What does **harks back** mean? _____

   _____

4. In Long Beach, California, you can visit an old Russian submarine from the Cold War era. Tours take you into many parts of the ship. You can see the torpedo room, the sleeping quarters, the old top-secret command center, and the **galley,** where food was prepared.

   What is a **galley?** _____

   _____

Read each passage. Circle the letter of the word that means about the same as that of the word in bold type. Use context clues.

Hikers in Glacier National Park in Montana

1. If it starts to rain, we may decide to **curtail** our hike. However, I'm willing to get an early start so that we can cover most of the trail while the weather is still fair.

    a. shorten   b. extend   c. film

2. Try to oil your baseball glove each week. This will keep the leather **supple,** which may prevent cracks and tears. It makes the glove easier to use, too.

    a. wet   b. clean   c. flexible

3. Our parents are always trying to make ends meet. They try not to spend too much money on most items. Yet they never **scrimp** on food. Mom says that a good diet will ensure a healthy mind in a healthy body.

    a. spend as little   b. complain   c. deposit money
    as possible

4. The metal smith makes beautiful jewelry from bronze, copper, silver, gold, and **platinum.** Of course, the platinum pieces are the most expensive.

    a. type of rock   b. an earring   c. a precious metal

5. The team whined and complained. They offered every excuse. Yet the coach remained **obstinate.** He refused to change his mind. He would not yield to any of the arguments.

    a. active   b. stubborn   c. flexible

6. Very few women wear fancy hats anymore, so the owner decided to close the **millinery** section of the department store. It just wasn't worth it to keep that department going.

    a. men's shoes   b. children's toys   c. ladies' hats

Extend & Apply

Gaunt means "very thin and bony, with hollow eyes and a starved look." Use this word in a sentence or a paragraph that gives context clues that suggest its meaning.

Name _____

A pioneer woman in a **pinafore**

⭐ **Each sentence compares two things. Read the sentence. Answer the questions that follow.**

1. Her light, sleeveless dress, which ties in the back, is similar to the **pinafore** that a pioneer woman often wore over her clothes.

    Which words show a comparison? _____

    What is a **pinafore?** _____

2. Saying that something is **gaudy** is the same as saying it is flashy and tasteless.

    Which words show a comparison? _____

    What does **gaudy** mean? _____

3. The **piquant** flavor of the sauce is just as sharp as my mom's spiciest tacos.

    Which words show a comparison? _____

    What does **piquant** mean? _____

4. We **vanquished** the Lions in much the same way that we defeated the Bears.

    Which words show a comparison? _____

    What does **vanquished** mean? _____

> **WORK TOGETHER**
>
> Work in a small group. Brainstorm a list of words or phrases that you might use to signal a comparison between two items.

⭐ **Figure out the meaning of the word in bold type. Use words that show a comparison in the sentence as context clues to help you.**

1. People **hastened** to Sutter's Mill when gold was discovered there in the same way that a dog rushes for a juicy bone.

   Hastened means _____.

2. The gate was as **unyielding** to our pushing as a wall of solid rock.

   Unyielding means _____.

3. Her look was as **serene** as the calmest lake I have ever sat by.

   Serene means _____.

4. His approach to life is just as **intrepid** as that of the brave heroes he admires.

   Intrepid means _____.

5. Jack London was as **productive** a writer as Babe Ruth was a hitter.

   Productive means _____.

6. In an earthquake, even sturdy buildings can **topple** like a house of cards.

   Topple means _____.

7. Hoover Dam **impounds** the waters of Lake Mead in the same way that a corral holds wild horses.

   Impounds means _____

   _____.

8. Her **melodic** voice sounds as rich as a lark's sweet song.

   Melodic means _____

   _____.

Hoover Dam

🏠 **Home Involvement Activity** A **simile** is a figure of speech that compares two unlike things by using the words **like**, **as**, or **than**. *She is **as** graceful **as** a swan.* Make up your own similes.

Name _____

> **Helpful Hint**

When you **contrast** two items, you show how they are different. You can get at the meaning of an unfamiliar word by noticing how two things contrast.

Miki says arugula tastes *unlike* other salad greens.

The word *unlike* signals that a contrast is being made. You can use this **context clue** to figure out that arugula is a kind of salad green.

A butte in Zion National Park, Utah

Each sentence contrasts two things. Read the sentence. Answer the questions that follow.

1. The walls of the butte are **crimson,** whereas few other landforms are red.

   Which word signals a contrast? _____

   What does **crimson** mean? _____

2. Meg is **prosperous,** but in contrast to millionaires, her wealth is modest.

   Which words signal a contrast? _____

   What does **prosperous** mean? _____

3. The guard was **vigilant;** otherwise, he would not have spotted the thief.

   Which word signals a contrast? _____

   What does **vigilant** mean? _____

4. My sister is often **morose,** as opposed to my brother, who is always cheerful.

   Which words signal a contrast? _____

   What does **morose** mean? _____

5. Carlos is **brawny,** although he is no weight lifter.

   Which word signals a contrast? _____

   What does **brawny** mean? _____

> **WORK TOGETHER**
>
> Work in a small group. Write five sentences, each contrasting two items. Then underline the words or phrases that signal a contrast.

Figure out the meaning of the word in bold type. Use words that signal a contrast in the sentence as context clues to help you.

1. Brixton is a **hard-boiled** rodeo star, but he has a soft spot for poetry and flowers.

   Hard-boiled means _____

   _____.

2. Instead of **gamboling** in the field with the other children, she sat nursing her sore ankle.

   Gamboling means _____

   _____.

A rodeo rider in Wyoming

3. The others climbed to the **belfry** while I stayed at the foot of the tower, listening for the bells.

   Belfry means _____.

4. He is **insolent;** on the other hand, all his classmates are courteous and respectful.

   Insolent means _____.

5. Unlike Ray, who is a **pessimist,** Courtney sees the brighter side of things.

   Pessimist means _____.

6. In contrast to the **robust** lifeguard at West Beach, the one here looks weak and thin.

   Robust means _____.

7. Danny is honest in his dealings with people, whereas Greg is disloyal and **deceitful.**

   Deceitful means _____.

8. Iris tried to **pacify** the baby; however, Rob did nothing to soothe the child.

   Pacify means _____.

Home Involvement Activity Use these words to create four sentences, each contrasting two things: **unlike, but, however,** and **while.**

Name _____

> **Helpful Hint**

Remember that you use **comparison** to show how two items are *alike.* You use **contrast** to show how two items are *different.*

Scene from the movie *The **Villain** Still Pursued Her,* 1940

⭐ **Each sentence compares *or* contrasts two things. Read the sentence. Underline the word *compare* or *contrast* to identify the kind of context clue being used. Then on the line, write the meaning of the word in bold type.**

1. The new dictator is as bad as any **villain** in a Hollywood movie.

   compare   contrast   **Villain** means _____.

2. My uncle is always **jovial,** whereas my aunt is usually serious.

   compare   contrast   **Jovial** means _____.

3. Saying that the troops **plundered** the town is the same as saying that they stole its goods.

   compare   contrast   **Plundered** means _____.

4. Tony's answer was **inane,** in contrast to my answer, which was sensible.

   compare   contrast   **Inane** means _____.

5. Marcos is as **arrogant** as his sister is humble.

   compare   contrast   **Arrogant** means _____.

6. There is no doubt that his **slander** of the candidate is similar to the lies he wrote about him in the newspaper.

   compare   contrast   **Slander** means _____.

7. Dad gives me **subtle** hints, while my mother is much more forceful and direct.

   compare   contrast   **Subtle** means _____

   _____.

> **CHALLENGE**
>
> Write two sentences that compare **and** two that contrast.

Figure out the meaning of the word in bold type. Use words that show comparison or contrast as context clues in the sentence.

Salt Lake City, Utah

1. Hatch, Utah, is a **hamlet;** on the other hand, Salt Lake City is a major urban area.

   Hamlet means _____

   _____ .

2. The mayor will try our plan, even though she is usually **skeptical** about new ideas.

   Skeptical means _____ .

3. She **flails** her arms about in the same way that people do in the water to attract the lifeguard.

   Flails means _____ .

4. Karen **garbles** her words, unlike Gabe, who speaks loudly and clearly.

   Garbles means _____ .

5. Similarly, her outfit was as **flamboyant** as her flashy new car.

   Flamboyant means _____ .

6. To say that I am **cynical** is the same as saying that I doubt and sneer at the things people say and do.

   Cynical means _____ .

7. Despite the **havoc** usually caused by hurricanes, this storm caused little damage.

   Havoc means _____ .

8. Some rain would be **beneficial** to our region, whereas too much would ruin the crops.

   Beneficial means _____ .

9. To spot the **elusive** gray wolf in the wild is equal to finding a four-leaf clover.

   Elusive means _____ .

LESSON 78: Context Clues—
Comparison and Contrast

Home Involvement Activity Find three hard words in a dictionary. Then use each word in a sentence that has **compare** or **contrast** clues. Challenge family members to figure out the meaning of the three words.

Name _____

Read each sentence. Then answer the questions that follow. You will need to make inferences based on context clues in the sentences.

1. Dad **swerved** off the road to avoid hitting a deer that had suddenly appeared.

   What was Dad doing? _____

   Therefore, what does it mean to **swerve?** _____

2. We want the best **orator** in our school to give the main speech at graduation.

   What traits should someone who gives an important speech have? _____

   _____

   Therefore, what is an **orator?** _____

3. We cleared away the **debris** on the beach so that we could have a clean, unspoiled spot for swimming.

   What would make a beach unclean or spoiled? _____

   Therefore, what is **debris?** _____

> **WORD STRATEGY**

An inference is an "educated guess." After you make an inference, go back to test your guess. Does it work in the sentence? Does it help you understand the meaning of the unfamiliar word? If not, try again.

Read each sentence. Choose the word or phrase from the box whose meaning matches the word in bold type. Write that word or phrase on the line.

agreement	hate	in spite of	touches	ordered
newness	on time	similar	unplanned	

1. The Montana State Fair in Great Falls attracts 200,000 visitors each year, **regardless of** how far people have to travel to get there.

   _____

2. They wound up playing an **impromptu** game of baseball with a broom and a bag of green apples.

   _____

   Great Falls, Montana

3. We **detest** war and will do everything we can to support the United Nations.

   _____

4. When Grandma **caresses** my face, she always strokes it gently.

   _____

5. It took hours of discussion and debate, but our group finally came to a **consensus.** _____

6. Try to be **punctual** for an interview, even if you think that the other person may be late. _____

7. He **commanded** his troops to retreat, but one soldier continued to fight.

   _____

8. After the **novelty** of the twist wore off, people quickly grew tired of this dance. _____

9. Ansel Adams and I are **kindred** spirits; we both admire the natural beauty of the West. _____

Home Involvement Activity Pick a Word of the Day. Family members can take turns introducing this new word and using it in a sentence. Be sure that the meaning of the word can be determined by context clues.

Name _____

> ## Helpful Hint
>
> Use **inference** to figure out the meaning of something not stated directly. This is the most common type of **context clue.**

Firefighters in Yellowstone National Park

⭐ **Read each sentence. Use inference to guess the meaning of the word in bold type. Then write the word in bold type next to the definition below that most closely matches its meaning.**

- A wild **inferno** left behind burned trees.

- Raccoons are **adept** at using their paws, which makes them good backyard thieves!

- Smooth talk may **beguile** you out of your money.

- Unfortunately, politicians don't often give their **candid** opinion about the issues.

- She is so creative that she can **cobble** together junk and make it look like art.

- Some superstars think that their fame lets them break the law without **penalty.**

- Science has **eradicated** some diseases and made others easy to treat.

- She used strength she didn't know she had to escape from the **rubble** caused by the earthquake.

_____ 1. gotten rid of forever

_____ 2. punishment

_____ 3. honest or frank

_____ 4. intense fire with great heat

_____ 5. put together roughly

_____ 6. pieces from ruined buildings

_____ 7. highly skilled

_____ 8. trick, cheat, deceive

> ## CHALLENGE
>
> In an analogy, relationships between words are unstated. Use inference to see the relationship in this analogy:
>
> **Juvenile** is to **mature** as **early** is to **late.**
>
> Tell how the ideas are connected.

Read each sentence about an amusing place name in the West. Use context clues, inference, and your own knowledge and experience to guess the meaning of the word in bold type. Then on the line, write a simple definition of the word.

1. It's fun to **speculate** about how Wisdom, Montana, may have gotten its name.

   speculate: _____

2. The naming of Riddle, Idaho, remains an **enigma** to this day.

   enigma: _____

3. I'll bet that the post office did not **inform** you that there is a Manhattan in the middle of Nevada!

   inform: _____

4. The folks in Utah may know whether you really can hear the **din** of billions of insects in the Cricket Mountains.

   din: _____

5. Let's guess why pioneers in Last Chance, Colorado, gave the town its **ominous** name.

   ominous: _____

6. If you wish to grow a lush garden, you might want to **acknowledge** that Weed, California, is not the place to buy land.

   acknowledge: _____

7. It's strange that my friend in Plain City, Utah, plans to build an **elaborate** house.

   elaborate: _____

8. A **chronicle** of the life and times of Story, Wyoming, should give you all the historical facts.

   chronicle: _____

9. Does the county have an **obligation** to build crooked roads in Bent County, Colorado?

   obligation: _____

LESSON 80: Context Clues—
Inference 2

Home Involvement Activity Refer to a map of your state. Make a list of interesting place names. Try to find out how each of these places got its name.

Name _____

Helpful Hints

You know that you can use context clues to unlock the meaning of words you don't know. There are several ways to do this:

Use your **experience.**
Look for a **definition** in the sentence.
Look for related **words in a series.**
Use clues to **compare** or **contrast.**
Make **inferences.**

James Beckwourth (1798–1867?)

⭐ **Read each passage. Fill in the circle of the word or words that have the same meaning as that of the word in bold type. Use context clues.**

1. Before the pioneers settled in the West, mountain men like Jim Bridger and James Beckwourth came. These trappers lived and hunted alone. Life in the wilderness was hard and dangerous. The trappers had to be tough. They had to show great **fortitude** in order to survive.
   - ○ wealth   ○ eagerness   ○ strength

2. Fort Laramie, Wyoming, was only a fur-trading post in 1834. Yet when the arrival of wagon trains was **imminent,** the fort took on a new role. It soon provided food, shelter, and protection to the pioneers.
   - ○ close at hand   ○ traveling   ○ far away

3. The restaurant featured singing waiters. The food cost money, but the entertainment was **gratis.**
   - ○ cheap   ○ free   ○ colorful

4. It is warm and sunny by the beaches in California. The salt air feels good, but it **corrodes** the metal on cars. The metal can gradually wear away.
   - ○ paints   ○ covers up   ○ eats away

5. Bo teaches in an elementary school in Billings, Montana. Most of his students live in the city. Unlike them, Bo lives in a **rural** area outside the city limits.
   - ○ urban   ○ country   ○ suburban

WORK TOGETHER

Explain to a partner the type of context clue you used to arrive at each correct answer.

⭐ **Figure out the meaning of the word in bold type. Use context clues to help you. Write the meaning of the word on the line.**

1. After the **demise** of the mine, the people in the town lost their jobs. However, a group of them set up an old miner's museum to attract visitors.

   Demise means _____.

2. The science museum displayed the **shale,** sandstone, and limestone found in the canyon walls and in the landforms of the area.

   Shale is a kind of _____.

3. The **belligerent** old prospector loved to quarrel with the other miners. He would pick a fight with anyone who crossed his path.

   Belligerent means _____.

4. We did a **superb** job on that science project. In our opinion, it was similar in quality to the outstanding work that real scientists do.

   Superb means _____.

5. When Lin decided to become a scientist, she knew she had found her **niche;** on the other hand, Suki has not yet found a career that suits her.

   A **niche** is a _____.

6. We tried several experiments to keep the cat away from our food, but our cat is very **persistent.** She keeps trying until she gets her way.

   Persistent means _____.

7. My nephew is a **bungler.** He botches up everything he does.

   A **bungler** is a _____.

8. The work that people did to build the first railroad across the nation was hard. It was boring, too. The work was pure **drudgery.**

   Drudgery is _____.

Workers on the transcontinental railroad, 1865

LESSON 81: Context Clues—
Mixed Strategies

 Home Involvement Activity Today, most cities boast excellent science museums. What would you see in such a museum? What would you like to see? Talk about it. Then plan a family outing to a science museum in your area.

Name _____

Read each group of words. Say and spell each word or phrase in bold type. Repeat the word or words. Then sort them by whether they signal a comparison or a contrast. Write the word or phrase in the correct box below.

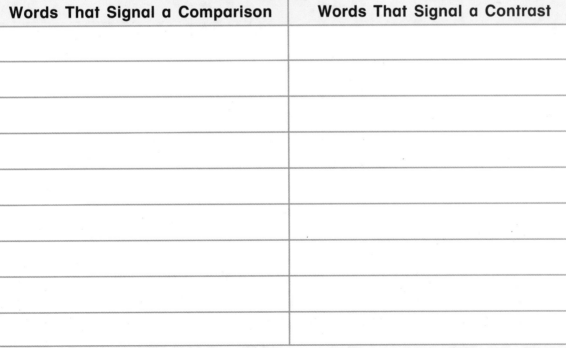

- so many **likenesses**
- a few **differences**
- **while** we aren't sure
- **despite** its differences
- **share** many features
- **although** it can't
- **alike** in several ways
- **compare** with mine
- **similar to** that fruit
- **instead of** buying
- behaves **similarly**

- **equal to** this
- **unlike** that
- **yet** they may not
- **both** seem to be
- **on the other hand**
- **by comparison**
- **by contrast**

San Francisco's Chinatown

Words That Signal a Comparison	Words That Signal a Contrast

Chinatown is a part of San Francisco. However, unlike the large Marina District, San Francisco's Chinatown is only seven blocks long and three blocks wide. Still, it attracts many visitors. More tourists come to this busy area than to the Marina. They like to visit the unusual restaurants and stores. Even the phone booths in Chinatown have a style all their own!

Choose two places to compare and contrast. Complete the chart below. List the features of each place in the outside boxes. In the middle box, list how the two places are alike. Later, use at least four of these words or phrases to write a comparison-contrast paragraph.

likenesses	differences	while	despite
share	although	alike	compare
similar to	instead of		similarly
equal to	unlike	yet	both
on the other hand	by comparison	by contrast	

Writer's Tip

You can organize your paragraph **point-by-point.** This lets you move back and forth between the two places, comparing one place then the other as you go.

Place #1

_____

_____

_____

Both Places

_____

_____

_____

Place #2

_____

_____

_____

_____

Writer's Challenge

Now compare your two places in a paragraph that compares and contrasts. Organize your writing in a way that makes sense. Use your spelling words to help you compare and contrast.

Name _____

⭐ **Read about an exciting adventure through Yellowstone National Park. Then answer the questions that follow.**

Snowmobile Safari!

by W. E. Butterworth IV

Old Faithful geyser erupting in Yellowstone National Park

Eagle Scout Peter Ivie gripped the snowmobile's passenger safety handles with all his strength. He leaned as the driver, Eagle Scout J.R. Fillmore, steered the machine into a snow-packed turn. The snowmobile's front skis found and followed an easy path.

"Go, go, go!" Peter encouraged, shouting to be heard over the engine and wind noises.

But just then, J.R. quickly throttled to idle. The snowmobile slid to a stop. Stepping onto the roadside— and into the boys' path—were a half-dozen bison.

J.R. and Peter looked at the mighty animals. One curious beast <u>ambled</u> toward their snowmobile. The boys turned to each other, exchanging wide-eyed expressions.

"Go, go, go!" both boys cried as J.R. turned the snowmobile in the opposite direction.

"We've run into a lot of wildlife," said Peter. "Well, not *run* into, but we've seen amazing animals."

"And scenery," J.R. added. "I've driven snowmobiles before, but never in such a beautiful wilderness area. I've never seen Yellowstone in winter. It's a whole different place."

Yellowstone National Park covers 2.2 million acres in Wyoming, Montana, and Idaho. Giant columns of hot water and steam, called "geysers," shoot up hundreds of feet. It's considered the world's greatest geyser area. And Old Faithful is Yellowstone's most famous geyser.

The Explorers were not sure if Old Faithful had been the trip highlight. Already the bison were getting bigger with each telling of the story!

⭐ 📖 Reader's Response

1. **The boys are impressed by the beauty of Yellowstone in the winter. How is it different from the park in the summer?**

2. **The writer says that one of the bison "ambled toward their snowmobile." What context clues helped you figure out what <u>ambled</u> means?**

3. **Imagine that you could speak with the boys in the story. What would you ask them? What would they say?**

Bison, elk, moose, deer, antelope, coyote—these are just some of the animals that the boys encountered on their snowmobile safari through Yellowstone National Park.

Now it's your turn. Choose two similar animals—such as an elk and a moose. Write a comparison-contrast essay showing how these two animals are similar, yet different. You can begin by making a chart to organize your essay. Include at least two of these words in your essay to show how your two animals are like and unlike each other.

Similarities:	like alike both also similar
	in the same way by comparison
Differences:	unlike different although while
	but yet however by contrast

Writer's Tip

You can organize your details **item-by-item.** This means presenting all the features of your first animal and then showing how your second animal is similar, yet different.

Bison in Yellowstone National Park

Writer's Challenge

Use "Snowmobile Safari!" for inspiration to create an observation chart of an animal you enjoy watching. Make a chart with two columns, labeled *Actions* and *Reasons.* First, observe and list the animal's actions. Then make inferences to guess why the animal responds in that way.

Name _____

Read each passage about northern California. Fill in the circle of the word that has the same meaning as that of the word in bold type. Use context clues to help you.

1. Sequoia trees, named for the Cherokee Sequoyah, grow in northern California. Some of the mature trees are more than 2,000 years old. These strong trees **thrive** in foggy areas where they can collect moisture on their needles.

   ○ do well   ○ weaken   ○ rot

2. Point Arena is a busy port town on the Pacific Coast. Fishing is its main source of income. The **wealthiest** merchants do well selling sea urchin, or *uni.* Japanese clients pay high prices for this salty treat.

   ○ most unusual   ○ smartest   ○ richest

3. Blue Lake might consider changing its name. The Mad River, which once fed Blue Lake, changed its direction. Now there is no more lake; instead, there is a squishy **bog** where the lake once was.

   ○ marsh   ○ beach   ○ forest

4. Have you been to the annual Slug Fest in Guerneville? This festival honors a local **inhabitant,** the banana slug. Banana slugs live in redwood forests. These slimy creatures look like bright yellow snails without shells.

   ○ hero   ○ resident   ○ festival

5. Some Native Americans honored Mount Shasta as a holy place. They believed that it was the home of the Great Spirit. To show respect, they never **ascended** higher than the tree line. This way, they would never disturb the Great Spirit's rest.

   ○ sang   ○ looked   ○ climbed

6. The llama is used as a pack animal for hikes in wilderness areas. Llamas are strong, calm, sure-footed, and do little to harm nature. They can nibble leaves and grasses as they **descend** a hiking trail. Northern California has several llama ranches.

   ○ go down   ○ go up   ○ move sideways

7. New York is called The Big Apple. Sacramento residents call their city The Big Tomato. This nickname **recalls** Sacramento's roots in farming.

   ○ excites   ○ brings back to mind   ○ removes

Read the passage. Fill in the circle of the answer to each question below.

Nellie Tayloe Ross
(1876–1977)

Wyoming has two nicknames—the Cowboy State and the Equality State. It is easy to guess how it got its first name. But do you know why it is called the Equality State?

In 1869, Wyoming wasn't a state yet. It was called the Wyoming Territory. Yet it was the first place in North America where women could legally vote. In those days, people had different ideas about women's rights than they do now. Back then, most men thought that women were unfit to vote. Yet Wyoming lawmakers did not agree with this **viewpoint.** They gave women full equality at the ballot box for local elections.

Wyoming became a state in 1890. Happily, its women kept their **suffrage.** Wyoming was a **model** for other Western states. Not long after, women **obtained** the right to vote in Utah, Colorado, Idaho, Montana, and Nevada. Wyoming is proud of its reputation as the Equality State. In fact, Nellie Tayloe Ross of Wyoming became the first female governor in the United States.

1. **Viewpoint** means ○ lesson ○ sight ○ position

2. **Suffrage** is the right to ○ vote ○ drive ○ marry

3. **Model** means ○ example ○ fashion ○ shape

4. **Obtained** means ○ fought ○ bought ○ got

Read the passage again. Circle the letter of the correct answer.

5. How did Wyoming lead other states?
   a. It had more cowboys.
   b. It had more people.
   c. Its land was richer.
   d. Its women could vote.

6. The ballot box is where
   a. farmers bale hay.
   b. people vote.
   c. judges live.
   d. the capital is.

Extend & Apply

You know what *divide* means in math. Yet you may not know what the *Continental Divide* is. Do research and then write an encyclopedia entry about the Continental Divide. Hint: You can see it in Yellowstone National Park.

"The Great Land"

Alaska and Hawaii were the last two United States territories to become states. Alaska became the forty-ninth state in 1959. A year later, Hawaii became the fiftieth state. In this unit, you will discover the natural beauty of our country's Pacific Northwest. You will also learn about Alaska and Hawaii, our nation's two youngest states.

The native people of Alaska were right when they called it *Alyeska,* which means "the great land." Alaska is twice the size of Texas. Within its 586,400 acres of wilderness there are 3 million lakes and 1,800 islands. There are 100,000 glaciers, 9 national parks, and 2 national forests.

The United States bought Alaska from Russia in 1867 for just two cents an acre. At the time, many thought that Secretary of State William Seward had made a bad deal. In fact, the Alaska purchase was called "Seward's Folly." Yet with this deal, the country gained a gorgeous frontier land, rich in oil, gold, fish, and timber.

Today, Alaska remains a feast for the eyes. Look up and you can see Mount McKinley, the tallest peak in North America. Look up even higher, to the night sky. There you may see dancing ribbons of red, white, blue, and green. These are the northern lights.

Critical Thinking

1. **How is Alaska a feast for the eyes?**

2. **Why was Seward's purchase called "Seward's Folly"? Was it foolish? Explain.**

3. **Close your eyes. What do you see when you think of Alaska? Draw a picture and write a caption.**

LESSON 85: Introduction to Dictionary and Thesaurus Skills; Synonyms, Antonyms, and Homonyms; Word Origin and Language Development

173

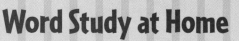

UNIT 6
Northwest & Hawaii

"The Great Land"

Alaska and Hawaii were the last two United States territories to become states. Alaska became the forty-ninth state in 1959. A year later, Hawaii became the fiftieth state. In this unit, you will discover the natural beauty of our country's Pacific Northwest. You will also learn about Alaska and Hawaii, our nation's two youngest states.

The native people of Alaska were right when they called it Alyeska, which means "the great land." Alaska is twice the size of Texas. Within its 586,400 acres of wilderness there are 3 million lakes and 1,800 islands. There are 100,000 glaciers, 9 national parks, and 2 national forests.

The United States bought Alaska from Russia in 1867 for just two cents an acre. At the time, many thought that Secretary of State William Seward had made a bad deal. In fact, the Alaska purchase was called "Seward's Folly." Yet with this deal, the country gained a gorgeous frontier land, rich in oil, gold, fish, and timber.

Today, Alaska remains a feast for the eyes. Look up and you can see Mount McKinley, the tallest peak in North America. Look up even higher, to the night sky. There you may see dancing ribbons of red, white, blue, and green. These are the northern lights.

Critical Thinking
1. How is Alaska a feast for the eyes?
2. Why was Seward's purchase called "Seward's Folly"? Was it foolish? Explain.
3. Close your eyes. What do you see when you think of Alaska? Draw a picture and write a caption.

LESSON 85: Introduction to Dictionary and Thesaurus Skills; Synonyms, Antonyms, and Homonyms; Word Origin and Language Development

173

Dear Family,

Your child has begun Unit 6. Lessons in this unit focus on dictionary and thesaurus skills; on synonyms, antonyms, and homonyms; on clipped, blended, and borrowed words; on eponyms and collective nouns; on idioms and analogies. The theme of this unit is the *Pacific Northwest, Alaska, and Hawaii,* including their people and history.

Synonyms are words that have the same or nearly the same meaning (**small** and **tiny**).

Antonyms are words that have opposite meanings (**small** and **large**).

Homonyms are words that sound the same but have a different meaning and a different spelling (**wood** and **would**).

Word analogies show how words and ideas are related. (**High** is to **low** as **big** is to **small.**)

Family Focus

- Read the nonfiction selection on page 173 and talk about it together. Have you ever been to Alaska? Would you like to visit the "Last Frontier"? If so, what would you want to see and do there?

- Obtain travel brochures for destinations in Hawaii and the Northwest, including Alaska. Plan a real or an imagined family trip.

- Keep a dictionary at hand. Make a list of the words you look up as you discover more about the people, history, and natural wonders of the places in this unit.

LINKS TO LEARNING

Web Sites
www.state.ak.us

www.everythingalaska.com

Videos
Denali: Alaska's Great Wilderness, part of *The Living Edens* series, PBS Home Video.

Explore Alaska: The Last Frontier, National Geographic Video, 3 videos.

Mount St. Helen's Fury, TLC Video.

Literature
A Day in the Life of Hawaii by David Cohen and Rick Smolan, 1984.

My Denali by Kimberly Coral, ©1995.

174

LESSON 85: Introduction to Dictionary and Thesaurus Skills; Synonyms, Antonyms, and Homonyms; Word Origin and Language Development—Word Study at Home

Name _____

Helpful Hint

Words in a dictionary are arranged in **ABC order,** or **alphabetical order.** To put words in ABC order, look at the first letter of each word. If the first letter is the same in each word, look at the next letter or letters to decide the ABC order of the words.

Read the names of these cities in Alaska, Hawaii, Washington, and Oregon. The names are arranged in ABC order.

Honolulu   Juneau   Pearl City   Portland   Salem   Seattle   Sitka   Tacoma

Write each group of words in ABC order.

1. admire   _____
   advance   _____
   artist   _____
   acre   _____
   arid   _____

2. rhythm   _____
   reunion   _____
   sweatshirt   _____
   suitable   _____
   rhyme   _____

Figure out this riddle. In each box, write the letter of the alphabet that comes *before* the letter given in the box. Then write the riddle's question and answer on the lines below. The first letter is given.

W														
X	I	B	U		E	P		Q	F	P	Q	M	F		E	P

J	O		P	S	F	H	P	O		X	I	F	O		J	U

					?									
S	B	J	O	T		M	F	U		J	U		S	B	J	O

Question: _____

Answer: _____

CHALLENGE

Teresa tasted many green grapes is a sentence with words in *reverse* **ABC order.** Create a similar sentence of your own. Make it as long as you can.

Write each group of words in ABC order.

1. ingredient _____
   indefinite _____
   illustrate _____
   kennel _____
   kernel _____

2. distort _____
   discourage _____
   divine _____
   diver _____
   dodge _____

3. warp _____
   wary _____
   wanderer _____
   wage _____
   warrior _____

4. past _____
   overcoat _____
   password _____
   partial _____
   outcry _____

All of these towns are in Alaska. Write their names in ABC order.

Kasigluk	Kwethluk	Kotzebue	Kiana	Kipnuk	Togiak
King Salmon	Kenai	Ketchikan	King Cove		Kasilof
Kotlik	Kodiak	Nulato	Kiawok		Hoonah

Welcome to Alaska's 1st City
KETCHIKAN
The Salmon Capital of the World

5. _____ 6. _____

7. _____ 8. _____

9. _____ 10. _____

11. _____ 12. _____

13. _____ 14. _____

15. _____ 16. _____

17. _____ 18. _____

19. _____ 20. _____

Home Involvement Activity Together, look at a map of your state. List 10 towns or cities. Challenge your family to put the places on your list in **ABC order.**

Name _____

Helpful Hint

Two **guide words** appear at the top of every dictionary page. They show the first and last **entry words** given on that page. The other words on the dictionary page appear in alphabetical order between those two guide words.

Read the guide words in bold type. Cross out two words on the list that would *not* be on the same dictionary page as the guide words. Then write the three other words in ABC order.

Narwhals

1   **nap / natural**
narwhal
nautical
napkin
nation
nameless

_____

_____

_____

2   **praise / precise**
prank
prince
prance
present
prayer

_____

_____

_____

3   **shack / shake**
shaky
shag
shaft
shark
shadow

_____

_____

_____

4   **current / curve**
cursor
curry
currency
cushion
curtain

_____

_____

_____

5   **bristle / broaden**
brood
broach
broadtail
brittle
broad

_____

_____

_____

WORK TOGETHER

Choose a partner. Ask each other riddles, such as: *I am a word found on a page with the guide words* **honk / hope.** *I am the sound that an owl makes. What am I?* Check your answer in a dictionary.

⭐ **Write each word from the box under the correct guide words below.**

shift	shallow	serve	serious
shimmer	shark	shatter	sesame	shield

1 series/session	**2** shale/shawl	**3** shell/shine
_____	_____	_____
_____	_____	_____
_____	_____	_____

⭐ **Read each sentence. Underline the word that would appear in a dictionary between the two guide words given at the left.**

frenzy/friend   4. Salmon are born in fresh water and then find their way to the ocean to grow.

saline/samba   5. Years later, mature salmon swim upstream to get back to their birthplace.

news/nibble   6. There, they spawn to begin the next new generation.

Fish ladder

fire/five   7. A few dams along natural salmon runs have blocked the fishways.

button/byway   8. One solution is to build a "fish ladder" to help salmon bypass the dams.

laundry/lead   9. A fish ladder is a series of pools in a step-by-step layout.

omit/ooze   10. The salmon can leap from one pool to the next in order to get over the dam.

tinsel/toad   11. Eddies provide rest areas for the tired fish.

Home Involvement Activity How many pages does your dictionary have? How many guide words? About how many entry words are there on a page? Do the math together. Use estimation.

Name _____

Helpful Hint

Think of the dictionary as having three parts.

The words in the **beginning** part start with the letters **A–I**.
The words in the **middle** part start with the letters **J–Q**.
The words in the **end** part start with the letters **R–Z**.

Turn to the beginning, the middle, or the end of the dictionary to locate words quickly.

Aerial view of Crater Lake

★ **Each sentence below has a word in bold type. Write *beginning, middle,* or *end* to tell in which part of the dictionary you would find that word.**

1. Crater Lake in Oregon is the deepest **lake** in the country. _____

2. It was formed about 7,700 years ago in a violent **volcanic** eruption. _____

3. The top 5,000 **feet** of what was once Mount Mazama collapsed. _____

4. Lava flow formed a sealed-off bowl called a **caldera.** _____

5. Rain and melted **snow** eventually filled the deep bowl, forming the lake. _____

★ **Sort the words about Crater Lake according to the part of the dictionary in which you would find them. Write each word in the correct column below.**

peak   lava   depth   ridge   crater   volcano   plateau   eruption   summit

6 **Beginning: A–I**	7 **Middle: J–Q**	8 **End: R–Z**
_____	_____	_____
_____	_____	_____
_____	_____	_____

CHALLENGE

Read the first activity again. Find another word in each sentence that would appear in the same part of the dictionary as that of the word in bold type.

Write *Beginning, Middle,* or *End* to tell in which part of the dictionary you would find each numbered word. Use A–I for the beginning part, J–Q for the middle part, or R–Z for the end part. Then underline the pair of guide words that would be on the same page as that ot the numbered word.

1. **exhibit** _____

   exhibitor / exotic   exempt / exist   excite / exhaust

2. **settlement** _____

   self / seminar   set / shade   slug / smear

3. **scenery** _____

   school / schwa   scare / scavenger   scene / scholar

4. **dignified** _____

   dignity / dime   diner / diorama   digital / dilute

5. **university** _____

   unity / unkindly   union / universe   unique / universal

6. **kilometer** _____

   kick / kiln   kidney / kimono   key / kilogram

7. **mountain** _____

   motor / mourn   mouth / Mozart   motel / mound

8. **summit** _____

   sultan / summarize   summary / sun   sunburn / super

9. **climb** _____

   climber / clock   clever / cliff   click / cling

Read the words in the box. Imagine that they are on one page of a dictionary and that two of them are guide words. Which would be the first guide word? Which would be the second?

| lanyard   land   lanky   landscape   language |

10. First guide word _____

11. Second guide word _____

Climber near top of
Mount Hood, Oregon

Home Involvement Activity Do a simple dictionary study. Which letter has the greatest number of entry words? The fewest? First, take a guess. Then find out together. Did anyone guess correctly?

Name _____

Helpful Hints

Words given in a dictionary are called **entry words.** Entry words appear in bold type in **ABC order.** The information about an entry word (its syllables, pronunciation, part of speech, definition, word history, and other forms of the word) is called the **entry.**

Many words that have **endings, prefixes,** or **suffixes** will not appear as separate entry words. You need to figure out the **base word** to know which entry word to look up.

surfer → **surf**   greatness → **great**

cleverly → **clever**   unshaken → **shake**

Surfer in Hawaii

★ **Read each word below. Write the entry word you would look up in the dictionary in order to find the word. Use a dictionary to help you.**

1. cleverness _____   2. generously _____

3. countries _____   4. gliding _____

5. clearer _____   6. forceful _____

7. independent _____   8. sprains _____

9. nonhuman _____   10. sharpness _____

11. reappear _____   12. carpenter _____

13. fulfillment _____   14. nicest _____

15. northern _____   16. silliness _____

17. debated _____   18. forgave _____

19. carelessness _____   20. unidentified _____

CHALLENGE

Write the **entry word** you would look up in the dictionary in order to find each of these words:

gratefully
inaccurately
nationalities

democracy A government in which the people rule directly, as through town meetings, or indirectly, through elected representatives.
de•moc•ra•cy (di mok′rə sē) *noun, plural* **democracies.**

demolish To tear down, destroy, or ruin completely. The workers will *demolish* the old library to make way for the new one.
de•mol•ish (di mol′ish) *verb.*

forsake To give up or desert completely. Do not *forsake* your old friends.
[Old English *forsacan,* to give up.]
for•sake (fôr sāk′) **-sook** (-sùk′), **-sak•en,** **-sak•ing** *verb.*

island A body of land completely surrounded by water.
is•land (ī′lənd) *noun.*

murky Dark or gloomy. The waters of the muddy river were *murky.*
murk•y (mûr′kē) **murk•i•er, murk•i•est** *adjective.* —**murk•i•ness** *noun.*

Read the dictionary entries for the five entry words above. Then write the entry word for each clue below.

1. This is what you do if you decide to give up or leave. _____

2. This is the fairest form of government. _____

3. Vancouver, British Columbia, which is off the southwestern coast of the mainland, is one of these. _____

4. This is how cloudy, thick pond water might look. _____

5. This is what you do if you destroy something completely. _____

Write your own sentence for each of the five entry words above.

6. _____

7. _____

8. _____

9. _____

10. _____

 Home Involvement Activity Suppose that the name of your street, county, and city or town appeared in a dictionary. Which entry word would appear just before? Just after? Look in a dictionary to find out.

Name _____

Helpful Hints

Many dictionaries have **entry words** for **contractions** and **abbreviations.** These entry words are listed in alphabetical order as if they were entire words.

All contractions have an **apostrophe** (**'**). But *not* all abbreviations have a **period** (**.**). Standard abbreviations may use all upper-case letters, all lower-case letters, or a combination of the two.

HI → Hawaii   **mi.** → mile   **km** → kilometer   **Dr.** → Doctor or Drive

Write the two words that each contraction stands for. Use a dictionary, if needed.

1. we've   _____ _____
2. who'll   _____ _____
3. you're   _____ _____
4. doesn't   _____ _____
5. I'm   _____ _____
6. didn't   _____ _____
7. let's   _____ _____
8. wouldn't   _____ _____
9. they're   _____ _____
10. won't   _____ _____

Write the word or words that each abbreviation stands for. Use a dictionary, if needed.

11. OR _____
12. AK _____
13. WA _____
14. lb. _____
15. P.S. _____
16. Mr. _____
17. doz. _____
18. pkwy. _____

WORK TOGETHER

Choose a partner. Write the **entry word** for each of these common abbreviations:

in.   oz.
pkg.   mph

Helpful Hint

Many dictionaries include entry words for acronyms. An **acronym** is a word formed from the first or first few letters of a series of words. Acronyms are listed in **ABC order** just as regular words are. Here are two acronyms:

NASA = **N**ational **A**eronautics and **S**pace **A**dministration

scuba = **s**elf-**c**ontained **u**nderwater **b**reathing **a**pparatus

Read each sentence. On the line below it, write the word or words that the abbreviation or acronym in bold type stands for. Use a dictionary to help you. Many abbreviations and acronyms are listed as entry words in the dictionary.

1. **NASA** maintains a large infrared telescope in Hawaii, called the Keck.

   _____

2. Hawaii has two official languages: **Eng.** and Hawaiian.

   _____

3. Hawaii has many fine spots that attract **scuba** divers.

   _____

4. Popular beaches get very crowded on **Sat.** afternoons.

   _____

5. My **ZIP** code in Honolulu is 96814.

   _____

Keck Telescope in Hawaii

6. Haleakala, Hawaii's largest volcano, rises more than 10,000 **ft.** above sea level.

   _____

7. We measured the Hawaiian flag in **in.**

   _____

8. Submarines in Hawaii use **sonar** to detect underwater objects.

   _____

Home Involvement Activity Each state has an official 2-letter postal abbreviation. For example, **HI** stands for Hawaii. How many of the post office abbreviations for the states do you know? Work together to try to list all fifty.

Name _____

Helpful Hints

Every dictionary has a **pronunciation key.**
This key appears at the beginning of the
dictionary and usually at the bottom of each
right-hand page. The pronunciation key uses
letters, symbols, and sample words to guide you
to say the sounds of the entry words.

Each dictionary entry gives a **respelling** of the
entry word, usually inside **parentheses ( ).** The
respelling uses the pronunciation key to show you
how to say the word.

bear (bâr)   book (bůk)   honey (hun'ē)

A caribou in Alaska's
Denali National Park

Pronunciation Key—Bottom of Dictionary Page

at; āpe; fär; câre; end; mē; it; īce; pîerce; hot; ōld; sông, fôrk; oil; out;
up; ūse; rüle; půll; tûrn; chin; sing; shop; thin; this; hw in white;
zh in treasure. The symbol ə stands for the unstressed vowel sound in
about, taken, pencil, lemon, and circus.

From the MACMILLAN SCHOOL DICTIONARY, © 1990,
reproduced with permission of The McGraw-Hill Companies.

Use the pronunciation key above to help you say each respelled word in
parentheses. Then write each word in the way it is usually spelled.
Use the words in the box below to help you.

| lounge | diary | enjoy | soar |

1. If you **(en joi')** seeing wildlife, then a trip
   to Alaska may be for you.   _____

2. Be sure to take binoculars and a
   (dī'ə rē) for writing notes.   _____

3. Watch the barking sea lions **(lounj)**
   on the beaches.   _____

4. See the falcons **(sôr)** above you. _____

CHALLENGE

Here are respellings
of the names of
three places. Write
the standard spelling
for each of the
names:

ə las´kə
ē´gəl
kō´dē ak´

Helpful Hint

The **pronunciation key** in the front of a dictionary shows the sound of each vowel and some consonants. Look at the pronunciation key below. It gives the sound of each vowel and sample words that have that vowel sound.

⭐ **Read each respelling below. Next to it, write the words from the pronunciation key that have the same vowel sound. Then give the usual spelling for the word. The first one has been done for you.**

A humpback whale flapping its tail

	Respelling	Example Words with Same Vowel Sound	Usual Spelling
1	(cou)	out, now	cow
2	(tāl)		
3	(stôr)		
4	(fôl)		
5	(kük)		
6	(spâr)		
7	(noiz)		
8	(nit)		
9	(fīr)		
10	(spül)		
11	(stûr)		
12	(fîrs)		
13	(rēth)		

Pronunciation Key—Front of Dictionary

a	at, bad
ā	ape, pain, day, break
ä	father, car, heart
âr	care, pair, bear, their, where
e	end, pet, said, heaven, friend
ē	equal, me, feet, team, piece, key
i	it, big, English, hymn
ī	ice, fine, lie, my
îr	ear, deer, here, pierce
o	odd, hot, watch
ō	old, oat, toe, low
ô	coffee, all, taught, law, fought
ôr	order, fork, horse, story, pour
oi	oil, toy
ou	out, now
u	up, mud, love, double
ū	use, mule, cue, feud, few
ü	rule, true, food
u̇	put, wood, should
ûr	burn, hurry, term, bird, word, courage
ə	about, taken, pencil, lemon, circus

Home Involvement Activity You can hear the **schwa sound (ə)** in many words. Work together to underline the vowel that makes the schwa sound in these words: **around, shaken, stencil, melon, custom.**

Name _____

Helpful Hints

When a word has two or more syllables, one syllable is **accented** more than the other syllable or syllables. You say the accented syllable with greater force, or stress.

In a dictionary respelling, look for an **accent mark (´)** *after* the accented syllable. This will help you say the word.

nation (**nā´shən**)   cascade (**kas kād´**)

Cascade at Olympic National Park in Washington State

Read each entry word. Then read the respelling in parentheses. Add an accent mark after the syllable you say with the greater or greatest force. Check a dictionary, as needed.

1. achieve   (**ə chēv**)   2. enemy   (**en ə mē**)

3. careful   (**kâr fəl**)   4. visible   (**viz ə bəl**)

5. vertical   (**vûr ti kəl**)   6. mountain (**moun tən**)

Helpful Hint

The same word may be pronounced in different ways, depending on its meaning or part of speech. The accent mark may shift to another syllable.

desert (**dez´ ərt**) → a dry, sandy region
desert (**di zûrt´**) → to leave someone or something

CHALLENGE

Check a dictionary. Find two meanings and pronunciations for **address.** Write a sentence using both meanings and pronunciations.

Read each sentence below. Underline the respelling of the word that best fits the meaning of the sentence.

7. I plan to _____ my Spanish on our trip.   (**pûr´ fikt**)   (**pər fekt´**)

8. Our class won the math _____ easily.   (**kon´ test**)   (**kən test´**)

9. Are you making _____ in class.   (**prog´ res**)   (**prə gres´**)

Complete each sentence with a word from the box. Some words will be used more than once. Then underline the respelling of the word in parentheses that matches the meaning of the sentence.

Hoh Rainforest in Olympic National Park

| entrance | perfect | present |
| record | refuse | subject |

1. The _____ of my paper is the Hoh Rainforest in Washington's Olympic Park. **(sub' jikt)** **(səb jekt')**

2. I took a trip there with my class. I kept a written _____ of everything I saw. **(rek' ərd)** **(ri kôrd')**

3. I used a pocket-sized notebook to _____ my observations. **(rek' ərd)** **(ri kôrd')**

4. The Hoh is a place that will _____ you. Nearly every bit of space is taken up with plants. **(en' trəns)** **(en trans')**

5. Let me _____ this fact. More than 12 feet of rain falls in the Hoh each year! **(prez' ənt)** **(pri zent')**

6. If people leave the trails, they may _____ the delicate environment to damage. **(sub' jikt)** **(səb jekt')**

7. Naturally, all visitors should take out with them any _____ that they may have brought in. **(ref' ūs)** **(ri fūz')**

8. Who could _____ to do that? **(ref' ūs)** **(ri fūz')**

9. I fully enjoyed my visit to the Hoh. I thought it was the _____ trip. **(pûr' fikt)** **(pər fekt')**

10. At the _____ to the Hoh, another tour group eagerly waited to begin its visit. **(en' trəns)** **(en trans')**

Home Involvement Activity Make a list of ten places in your community that you and your family visit each week. Use the pronunciation key and accent marks from a dictionary to respell the names of these places.

Name _____

Read each of the phrases below. Say and spell each word in bold type. Repeat the word. Then sort the words according to where you would find them in a dictionary. Write each word in the correct column below.

- gave a helpful **example**
- some **knowledge** of Japanese
- **research** its meaning
- the **standard** spelling
- help **pronounce** the word
- in **alphabetical** order
- an **unusual** word history
- longest **entries** in the book
- **abbreviate** the title
- forming a **contraction**
- **separate** into syllables
- learn a new **language**
- in the middle **section**
- **capitalize** your name

- the **origin** of the word
- so easy to **misspell**
- to **visualize** the word
- the **meaning** of the phrase

Beginning: A–I	Middle: J–Q	End: R–Z

SPELL & WRITE

You know that like a dictionary, an encyclopedia is a reference work. You have probably used a print or an on-line encyclopedia to do research. Encyclopedias have general articles, or entries, on many subjects. Like a dictionary, these articles appear in ABC order. A few encyclopedias are on special subjects, such as baseball. Some encyclopedias are just for children.

Write an article for a children's encyclopedia. Your topic is the *dictionary*. Give the key facts. Imagine that students in a younger grade will be reading your article to learn what a dictionary is and how to use it. Include a sample dictionary entry. Use at least two of these spelling words in your encyclopedia article.

example	knowledge	research	standard	pronounce
alphabetical	unusual	entries	abbreviate	contraction	separate
language	section	capitalize	origin	misspell	visualize	meaning

_____

_____

_____

_____

_____

_____

_____

_____

_____

Writer's Tips

- When you revise your writing, cross out any unimportant details.

- Add any important information that you may have left out.

Speaker's Challenge

Look up the word **research** in two different dictionaries. Compare and contrast the definitions. How are they alike? How are they different? Which meaning is easier to understand? Discuss your findings with a group.

Name _____

⭐ **Read about the Hawaii of yesterday and today.
Then answer the questions that follow.**

Hawaii—Then and Now

by Marcie and Rick Carroll

THEN

Thousands of years ago, people sailed across the Pacific Ocean to see what they could find. They found Hawaii—a string of islands in the middle of nowhere. This new place had erupting volcanoes, roaring shorelines, lots of birds, beautiful flowers, and thick tropical forests. Early settlers made themselves at home in the new territory and soon created their own language, customs, and traditions. Historians don't really know what island life was like in the beginning, because most ancient Hawaiian history is told either in old chants (sung in the Hawaiian language), or in unusual symbols and drawings that were carved into rocks long ago.

NOW

Today you'll find 1.1 million people living on the islands of Hawaii. You'll find cars, computers, film crews, and even the largest telescope in the world! Visit the city of Honolulu and you'll spot high-rise buildings, hotels, and hundreds of tourists arriving every day to check out the island life. Today, Hawaii may look a lot different than it did when the first settlers arrived, but many things haven't really changed. The air still smells like tropical flowers, the volcanoes are still erupting, the beaches are still golden, and the islands are still full of nooks and crannies to explore. Even ancient traditions—like hula, leis, and luaus—are still a big part of Hawaii. Aloha!

📖 Reader's Response

1. **What was Hawaii like when the first settlers arrived thousands of years ago?**

2. **How has Hawaii changed? Give three examples.**

3. **What do you think is the one most important thing that hasn't changed in Hawaii? Explain your choice.**

READ & WRITE

The first European explorers who came to Hawaii were astonished to see Hawaiians gracefully riding waves on long, carved wooden boards. The explorers were fascinated by this sport, which the Hawaiians called *he'enalu* (to "slide on a wave"). Like surfing, many things in Hawaii have stayed the same for hundreds or thousands of years. Plants, flowers, trees, birds, fish, and sea mammals still thrive in this tropical paradise. Yet high-rise hotels and apartment buildings, tourists, and traffic jams have brought many changes to the Hawaiian way of life.

Now it's your turn. Close your eyes. Visualize what you were like five years ago. Then think about how you have changed. Consider your appearance, your knowledge, your likes and dislikes, your daily activities, your responsibilities, and your new friends. Jot down your findings. Use your notes to write a then-and-now paragraph about you. Use at least two of these words or phrases.

Surfboard—then

personal	history	grown	appearance	know
responsibilities	relationships		similar	different
like	unlike	but	yet	by contrast

THEN _____

_____

_____

NOW _____

_____

_____

Writer's Tips

- In the **THEN** section, describe what you were like five years ago.

- In the **NOW** part, describe how you have changed.

- Include "then" and "now" photos of you.

Writer's Challenge

Think of a place you know or would like to know more about. Do some research. Describe what this place was like at some point in the past. Then tell what it is like today. Check a dictionary to see if you have used your words correctly.

Surfboard—now

Name _____

Read each group of words. Fill in the circle of the words
that appear in ABC order.

1	○ break freeze Greece juice ○ hornet horse husband hurry ○ west wrist willow zero	2	○ crush brush plush thrush ○ gnome gorgon dragon flagon ○ cracker crockery crook crystal
3	○ dawn morning midday sunset ○ although after afterward shortly ○ gargle giggle gurgle jangle	4	○ draft drain drift drench ○ frown laugh smirk snarl ○ iron immature inning itchy
5	○ imitate initial invitation interest ○ lavender lettuce licorice lotus ○ spend scream steam stream	6	○ Oregon oregano organ orange ○ hawk Hawaii hawthorn hayseed ○ quack quarter question quicken
7	○ phase phrase praise prance ○ tickle ticklish ticket tidy ○ over overlook overtake oven	8	○ unbuckle uncle unclear undergo ○ value valley valiant vanquish ○ yearly yeast yellow yawn
9	○ ocean o'clock October octopus ○ point poem poet palm ○ weather whether whale wail	10	○ mast mist misty mistletoe ○ lead leaky lei luau ○ ukulele uncle ulcer under

Each of the entry words in bold type is a fruit that grows in Hawaii.
Read each entry word. Underline the pair of guide words that would
appear on the same dictionary page as that of the entry word.

11. **coconut**	cobble/cocoa	cobbler/cocoon	code/coffee
12. **banana**	ball/band	bandit/bangle	bank/bark
13. **papaya**	papyrus/parakeet	palm/papa	pantry/paper
14. **pineapple**	pile/pinch	pilot/pinto	pink/pipe
15. **mango**	mane/manicure	mandolin/mangle	mangy/manner

Rewrite the five entry words above in alphabetical order.

16. _____ _____ _____ _____ _____

The words below name some of Oregon's important crops and products. Underline *beginning, middle,* or *end* to tell in which part of the dictionary you would find each word. Use A–I for the beginning, J–Q for the middle, or R–Z for the end.

1. lumber   beginning   middle   end

2. semiconductor   beginning   middle   end

3. paper   beginning   middle   end

4. hay   beginning   middle   end

5. electronics   beginning   middle   end

6. onion   beginning   middle   end

7. mint   beginning   middle   end

8. cement   beginning   middle   end

9. wheat   beginning   middle   end

10. pear   beginning   middle   end

Columbia River Gorge in Oregon

Read each sentence. Underline the respelling that fits the meaning of the word in bold type.

11. Oregon's nickname is the **Beaver** State.   (bē′ vər)   (bē vər′)

12. Its moderate **climate** makes it a popular place in which to live.   (klī mit′)   (klī′ mət)

13. Mount Hood is the **perfect** spot for outdoor activities.   (pûr′ fikt)   (pər fekt′)

14. I live **close** enough to the sea to hear the whales.   (klōz)   (klōs)

15. The Columbia River **Gorge** is deep.   (jôrj)   (gôrj)

Extend & Apply

Use a dictionary to look up the meanings of these words: **canyon, gorge,** and **valley.** How are the meanings of these words the same? How are they different? Write your answer.

Name _____

> ## Helpful Hint

Synonyms are words that have the same or nearly the same meaning.

make—create   worth—value   high—lofty

⭐ In each box, match the words in the first column with their synonyms in the second column.

1			2		
	love	demonstrate		dwell	conceal
	show	adore		hide	live
	frank	honest		mend	heal
3	error	respond	**4**	couple	provide
	answer	yell		supply	frequently
	shout	mistake		often	pair

Totem pole in Alaska

⭐ In each group of words below, one word does not belong. Cross out that word. Then explain on the lines why the word does not belong in the group.

5. say   state
rejoice   remark

_____

_____

6. thief   detective
crook   robber

_____

_____

7. attack   terrify
frighten   alarm

_____

_____

8. omit   restore
delete   remove

_____

_____

9. idea   thought
concept   energy

_____

_____

10. fragile   delicate
hazardous   breakable

_____

_____

> ### WORK TOGETHER

Form a small group. Work together to list as many **synonyms** for **big** and **small** as you can. Take 5 minutes. Compare your lists with those of another group.

Read the sentences below. Replace each word in bold type with a synonym from the box. Write the synonym on the line.

| reside | provide | summit | visitors | active | numerous |

1. Thousands of **tourists** explore Mount Rainier National Park each year. _____

2. The **peak** of Mount Rainier is always covered in snow. _____

3. People who **live** in the city of Tacoma are only a short drive from Mount Rainier National Park. _____

4. Each day, **many** ferries leave Seattle, Washington, for the San Juan Islands. _____

5. People in the city of Seattle may spend several hours at the **lively** Pike Place Market. _____

6. One of the uses of the Grand Coulee Dam in Washington State is to **supply** power. The dam is also used for irrigation and flood control. _____

Each scrambled word is a synonym for the word next to it. First, read the word. Then unscramble the letters in bold type. Write the unscrambled word on the line.

7. injure   **downu** _____

8. slim   **redslne** _____

9. empty   **vactan** _____

10. beginner   **earnrel** _____

11. income   **gniaersn** _____

12. victor   **napoimhc** _____

13. agree   **contnes** _____

14. reduce   **snelse** _____

Grand Coulee Dam

196   LESSON 96: Synonyms

Home Involvement Activity Parts of the Pacific Northwest get a great deal of rainfall. Therefore, plants and trees grow very tall in this region. Work together to list as many synonyms as you can for the word **tall**.

Name _____

Antonyms are words that have the opposite or nearly the opposite meaning.

powerful—weak   gain—lose   many—few

⭐ **Each row has three antonyms for each numbered word. Underline the three antonyms in each row.**

1. **give**	receive	grant	take	get
2. **healthy**	unhealthy	ill	fit	sick
3. **permanent**	unstable	short-lived	temporary	everlasting
4. **funny**	gloomy	depressing	amusing	sad
5. **polite**	courteous	discourteous	impolite	rude

⭐ **Read each sentence. Replace the word in bold type with its antonym from the box. Write the word on the line.**

dull   saved   closed   left   raised

_____ 6. You can see the **sunken** hull of the USS *ARIZONA* in Pearl Harbor.

_____ 7. The battleship *Arizona* was **destroyed** during World War II.

_____ 8. The United States **entered** the war after the ship was sunk.

_____ 9. Today, the *Arizona* Memorial in Hawaii is **open** to tourists.

_____ 10. A helicopter ride over Pearl Harbor can be a **thrilling** experience.

Arizona Memorial in Hawaii's Pearl Harbor

WORK TOGETHER

Form a small group. Work together to list all the **antonyms** you can think of for the words **wet** and **dry**. Which list will be greater?

Copyright © by William H. Sadlier, Inc. All rights reserved.

LESSON 97: Antonyms   **197**

Write an antonym from the box for each numbered clue below. Write one letter in each space. Then read down the shaded column to answer the question at the bottom.

begin	rude	healthy	asleep	seldom	major	quiet
uneven	forgive	front	most	hero	straight

1. sick _ _ _ _ _ _ _

2. minor _ _ _ _ _ _

3. noisy _ _ _ _ _

4. awake _ _ _ _ _ _

5. blame _ _ _ _ _ _ _

6. least _ _ _ _

7. back _ _ _ _ _

8. crooked _ _ _ _ _ _ _ _

9. coward _ _ _ _ _

10. level _ _ _ _ _ _

11. often _ _ _ _ _ _

12. polite _ _ _ _

13. finish _ _ _ _ _ _

Question: Haleakala National Park is in the eastern part of the Hawaiian island of Maui. It is named for the awesome Haleakala volcano. From the edge of the volcano's crater you can see several other islands. This special park has a nickname. What is it?

Answer: _____

Haleakala Crater

Home Involvement Activity Mauna Kea is the highest point in Hawaii. Alaska's highest point is Mt. McKinley. Find out the highest point in your state. How does it compare with the tallest peaks in Alaska and Hawaii?

Name _____

> **Helpful Hint**

Homonyms are words that sound alike but have different meanings and different spellings.

dear—deer   pause—paws   flower—flour

⭐ **Write the homonym from the box for each numbered word below.**

doe	tacks	beat	principle	crews	reel
steak	aloud	towed	boar	ceiling	passed

1. tax _____
2. beet _____
3. bore _____
4. sealing _____
5. cruise _____
6. dough _____
7. allowed _____
8. real _____
9. past _____
10. principal _____
11. toad _____
12. stake _____

> **CHALLENGE**
>
> **I'll, isle,** and **aisle** are a set of *three* homonyms. How many other sets of three homonyms can you think of? Make a list.

⭐ **Choose the homonym in parentheses that completes each sentence. Write the word on the line.**

13. Our (tour, tore) group was welcomed at the airport. _____

14. We will hike up Diamond Head (whether, weather) or not you join us. _____

15. Try to guess how much a humpback whale (ways, weighs). _____

16. It is an honor to be a (guessed, guest) at Iolani Palace, the only palace in the United States. _____

17. They (threw, through) a party on King Kamehameha Day. _____

18. I snorkeled along a (choral, coral) reef. _____

19. Will you (surf, serf) at Sunset Beach tomorrow? _____

Underline the pair of homonyms in each sentence. Then write a definition of each homonym. Use a dictionary, if needed.

1. It is eerie to hear the wail of a lonely whale in the harbor.

   _____

   _____

2. The meeting of the tenants' board bored me to tears.

   _____

   _____

3. Please do not meddle in our plans for the medal ceremony.

   _____

   _____

4. Among the loot the thieves took from the music shop were a trumpet and a lute.

   _____

   _____

5. I hope that our meeting won't last longer than an hour.

   _____

   _____

6. The messy child smeared grape jam on the door jamb near the kitchen.

   _____

   _____

7. At the war memorial, Uncle Joe wore his old Army uniform.

   _____

   _____

8. I have told you many times not to rub your eye.

   _____

   _____

Home Involvement Activity *Did you know the* gnu *that* Drew knew*?* is a funny sentence that uses a pair of homonyms. Create at least five funny sentences with homonym pairs.

Name _____

> **Helpful Hint**

An **entry word** with more than one meaning is called a **multiple-meaning word.** Each of the different meanings for that entry word is numbered.

Read each dictionary entry. Then read the sentences below it. On the line, write the number of the definition that fits the meaning of the word as it is used in the sentence.

clumsy 1. Awkward; not skillful or graceful. She is too *clumsy* to be a good gymnast. **2.** Awkwardly made or shaped. The *clumsy* gate kept hitting the bushes. **3.** Said or done without skill. His *clumsy* sentences were all the same length.

_____ **1.** We need a piece of wood to prop the **clumsy** window open.

_____ **2.** Don't use **clumsy** phrases in a poem!

_____ **3.** Their routine is too **clumsy** to be chosen for the dance solo.

endure 1. To undergo and survive; stand; bear. The first European explorers to come to the Americas had to *endure* many hardships. **2.** To continue to be; last. Mozart's music will *endure* forever.

_____ **4.** A beloved film like *The Wizard of Oz* will **endure** for generations to come.

_____ **5.** Grandpa told us of the many dangers he had to **endure** when he was a soldier.

issue 1. The act of sending or giving out. I was in charge of the *issue* of supplies to all the students. **2.** Something that is sent or given out. Do you have this month's *issue* of the magazine? **3.** A matter that is under discussion or consideration. The council debated the *issue* of raising local taxes.

_____ **6.** Pictures of Eugene, Oregon, appear in this month's **issue** of *Pacific* magazine.

_____ **7.** Recycling was the **issue** under debate.

_____ **8.** That librarian is in charge of the **issue** of new library cards.

> **WORD STRATEGY**

Multiple-meaning words may act as different parts of speech. What does each word mean as a noun? As a verb?

back
level
slump

Helpful Hint

Homographs are words that have more than one dictionary entry. Homographs are spelled the same but have different meanings. They may or may not sound alike. You can identify homographs in a dictionary by the small raised number that follows them. Here is a pair of homographs:

dove[1] Any small bird belonging to the pigeon family. A white *dove* is a symbol of peace.

dove[2] A past tense of **dive**. The swimmer *dove* from the cliff into the lake.

Cliff diver at Waimea Falls in Hawaii

Read the list of homographs and their meanings. **Then decide which word to use to complete each sentence below. Write the word and its number on the line.**

down[1]	From a higher to a lower place.	**mole**[1]	A small brown spot on the skin.
down[2]	Fine, soft feathers.	**mole**[2]	A small animal with fur and long claws that burrows holes underground.
grate[1]	Framework of bars set in or over an opening.	**spell**[1]	To write or say the letters of a word in order.
grate[2]	To make a scraping sound by rubbing.	**spell**[2]	State of being enchanted or fascinated.
		spell[3]	A period of time.

1. "Don't _____ your teeth," the dentist warned.

2. That region had a hot, dry _____ last summer.

3. A jacket filled with goose _____ will be warm and lightweight.

4. The _____ that lives in our backyard has ruined our lawn.

5. I can't resist the _____ of Italy—its music and art are enchanting.

6. We took the dusty stairs _____ to the storage room in the basement.

7. At night a _____ goes over the door to prevent looting.

8. Dad grew a beard to cover up the _____ on his chin.

9. Some people find long Hawaiian words and names hard to _____.

LESSON 99: Multiple-Meaning Words and Homographs

Home Involvement Activity Write two sentences for each of these homographs: **rock, slide, pitcher,** and **handle.** Then compare how you used these multiple-meaning words.

Name _____

⭐ **Choose a synonym for the word** *throw* **that best fits the movement shown in each picture. Use the words from the thesaurus entry below. Do not use a word more than once.**

throw [*v*] cast, chuck, flick, fling, heave, hurl, launch, lob, pelt, pitch, scatter, shower, thrust, toss, volley
Ant catch, receive

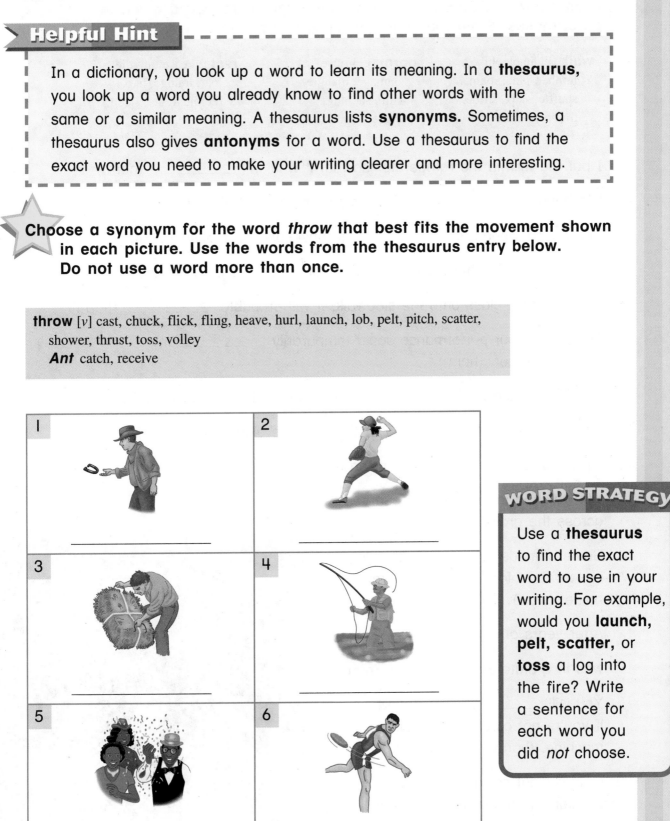

WORD STRATEGY

Use a **thesaurus** to find the exact word to use in your writing. For example, would you **launch, pelt, scatter,** or **toss** a log into the fire? Write a sentence for each word you did *not* choose.

⭐ **Read the synonyms for each of the three entry words below. Then read each sentence. Choose the best synonym for the word given in parentheses. Write the synonym on the line.**

walk [v] amble, hike, lumber, plod, roam, shuffle, stalk, stride, tramp, wander

harm [v] bruise, damage, mangle, ruin, sabotage, shatter, spoil, trample

rest [v] ease up, idle, loaf, lounge, nap, recline, relax, sleep

1. I put the milk in the refrigerator so that it wouldn't_____. (harm)

2. We began to _____ up the steep mountain trail. (walk)

3. The sly cat began to _____ the unsuspecting mouse. (walk)

4. To _____ after studying, I went for a swim in the lake. (rest)

5. If you drop a glass onto the sidewalk, it will probably _____. (harm)

6. One more poor performance could temporarily _____ the athlete's career. (harm)

7. The holiday crowds _____ the grass and the flower beds. (harm)

8. The spies worked to _____ the enemy's plans. (harm)

9. I plan to _____ for about ten minutes; please don't wake me. (rest)

10. We watched the clumsy old bear _____ across the gravel. (walk)

11. Some nomads _____ the desert in search of food and a temporary home. (walk)

12. After years of dry weather, the land was in a state of _____. (harm)

13. You will _____ your hand if you're not careful with that machine. (harm)

14. Only a giant could _____ through the forest like that. (walk)

Home Involvement Activity Become a "family thesaurus." Together, list as many synonyms as you can for the word **see.**

Name _____

Helpful Hint

A **thesaurus** lists synonyms and antonyms. Entry words in a thesaurus are arranged in **ABC order,** just as they are in a dictionary.

The box below has synonyms from a thesaurus for the words *slow*, *heavy*, and *fast*. Sort the words by their meaning. Write each word in the correct column below.

brisk	bulky	hefty	sluggish	snaillike	huge
dull	quick	overweight	swift	massive	hasty	gradual
unhurried	burdensome	accelerated	rapid	slack

1 slow	2 heavy	3 fast
_____	_____	_____
_____	_____	_____
_____	_____	_____
_____	_____	_____
_____	_____	_____

Rank each set of words from *least* to *most.* Write the words in the correct order on the line.

4. from *least* happy to *most* happy: pleased, elated, cheerful

_____

5. from *least* sad to *most* sad: sorrowful, gloomy, heartbroken

_____

6. from *least* cold to *most* cold: frosty, crisp, cool

_____

WORK TOGETHER

Get together with a partner. Write one more synonym for each word in items 4–6. Where would you rank your word in the list? Explain your decision.

Replace each word in bold type with a more exact word from the box. Use a word only *once*.

snaillike	overweight	brisk	swift	accelerated
massive	rough	hasty	bulky	slack

1. The very bright student was placed in a(n) **fast** class. _____

2. A **heavy** boulder blocked the road, so we couldn't pass. _____

3. The sleek and **fast** cheetah can run faster than almost any other animal. _____

4. Business was **slow;** we had no customers at all after two o'clock. _____

5. The **fast** decision we made may come back to haunt us. _____

6. The **heavy** dieter was shedding 10 pounds a week! _____

7. Business was **fast** in the first month. It slowed down after that. _____

8. The committee moves at a **slow** pace. _____

9. It was awkward to carry the **heavy** package up the stairs. _____

10. You can get from Seattle to Vancouver, Canada, by ferry if the sea is not too **heavy.** _____

Choose any three words from the box above. Use each word in a sentence that makes the meaning of the word clear.

11. _____

_____

12. _____

_____

13. _____

_____

Passengers aboard a Seattle ferry

Home Involvement Activity Use three words from the box at the top of the page to describe doing chores at your house. Give everyone a chance to contribute. Choose one person to write the description.

Name _____

⭐ **Read each pair of words. Write S if the words are *synonyms*. Write A if the words are *antonyms*. Write H if the words are *homonyms*.**

1. dwell—live _____
2. mist—missed _____
3. bore—boar _____
4. omit—delete _____
5. supply—provide _____
6. conceal—hide _____
7. gain—lose _____
8. polite—rude _____
9. strong—weak _____
10. ceiling—sealing _____
11. aisle—I'll _____
12. partial—complete _____
13. slender—thin _____
14. lessen—reduce _____
15. paws—pause _____
16. pedal—peddle _____
17. annoy—bother _____
18. distant—nearby _____
19. week—weak _____
20. crooked—straight _____
21. tacks—tax _____
22. often—frequently _____

⭐ **The box below has words from a thesaurus. Sort the words by their meaning. Write each word in the correct column below.**

bake	boil	bound	broil
consider	decide	grill	spring
leap	ponder	reason	vault

CHALLENGE

Replace the word in bold type with both a **synonym** and an **antonym**. All phrases should make sense.

skinny clown
loud **laugh**
damp weather

23 Words for **jump**	24 Words for **cook**	25 Words for **think**
_____	_____	_____
_____	_____	_____
_____	_____	_____
_____		

Underline the synonym for each word in bold type.

1. made too many **errors**   mistakes   calls   excuses

2. **grateful** for your kindness   angry   bored   thankful

3. **frighten** the audience   entertain   charge   scare

4. the newest **champion**   victor   loser   player

5. **numerous** activities for kids   many   few   math

Underline the antonym for each word in bold type.

6. **receive** birthday cards   send   get   buy

7. too **sweet** for my taste   crunchy   sugary   sour

8. **east** of the lake   north   west   outside

9. plays in the **major** leagues   minor   soccer   student

10. **seldom** has dessert   never   often   rarely

The sentences below are about the Oregon Trail. The pioneers traveled this trail on their way to the West. Choose the homonym that makes sense in the sentence. Write the word on the line.

11. There was no easy _____ to the West.   root   route

12. The trip took months in all kinds of _____.   weather   whether

13. The Oregon Trail was once a main _____ west.   rowed   road

14. It went _____ Wyoming and Idaho.   threw   through

Extend & Apply

Use a thesaurus to revise sentences 11–14. Change one word in each sentence. Choose a word that is more interesting or exact, but do *not* change the meaning of the sentence.

The Oregon Trail
- City
- Fort
- Trail
- Pass

Ft. Vancouver Washington
Oregon City
Oregon
Ft. Boise
Idaho
South Pass Ft. Laramie
Nebraska
Wyoming Ft. Kearny
Ft. Bridger
Kansas
Independence, Missouri

Name _____

Helpful Hint

Language changes all the time as people use it. Sometimes, long words get shortened so that they are easier to say and spell. These shorter forms are called **clipped words.** Here are some clipped words:

gymnasium → **gym**   automobile → **auto**   photograph → **photo**

⭐ **Match each clipped word in Column A with the long form of the word in Column B. Write the long form of the word on the line.**

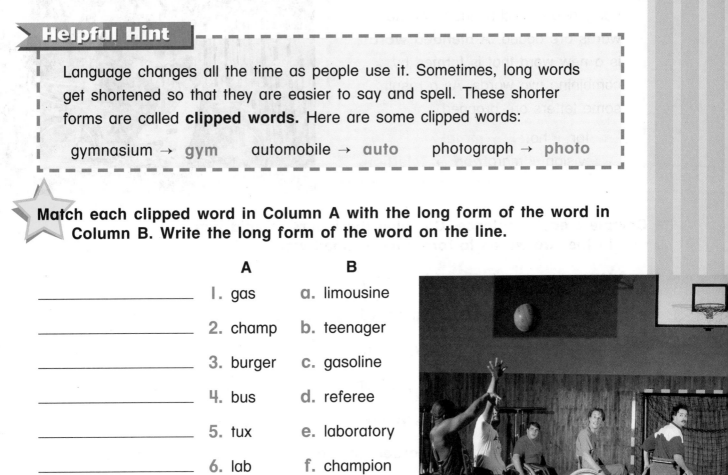

gymnasium → **gym**

	A	**B**
_____	1. gas	a. limousine
_____	2. champ	b. teenager
_____	3. burger	c. gasoline
_____	4. bus	d. referee
_____	5. tux	e. laboratory
_____	6. lab	f. champion
_____	7. ref	g. hamburger
_____	8. limo	h. omnibus
_____	9. teen	i. tuxedo

⭐ **Read the sentences. Replace each word in bold type with the clipped form of the word in the box. Write the clipped word on the line.**

vet	ad	taxi	grad

10. I cut out an **advertisement** from the newspaper. _____

11. My cousin is a recent **graduate** of that university. _____

12. Dawn took her cat to see the **veterinarian.** _____

13. They rode home in a **taxicab.** _____

CHALLENGE

What are the long forms of these clipped words? Use a dictionary to help you find and spell your answers.

flu

memo

sax

Language also changes when new words are added. A **blended word** is a new word that is formed by combining two words. As a result, some letters are dropped.

motor + hotel → motel
television + marathon → telethon

motor + pedal → moped

Complete each sentence. Combine the letters in bold type in the two words to form one blended word.

1. If you blend **mo**tor + **ped**al, you get _____.

2. If you blend **br**eakfast + **lunch,** you get _____.

3. If you blend **fl**utter + **h**urry, you get _____.

4. If you blend **sm**oke + f**og,** you get _____.

5. If you blend **fl**ame + gl**are,** you get _____.

6. If you blend **cam**era + re**corder,** you get _____.

7. If you blend **gl**eam + sh**immer,** you get _____.

8. If you blend **info**rmation + com**mercial,** you get _____.

Write one of the blended words from above to complete each sentence.

9. We saw the first _____ of light on the horizon at 5:00 A.M.

10. They served eggs, sausages, muffins, and fruit for _____.

11. A _____ of wind upset the small boat.

12. We took our new _____ to film our vacation.

13. The city in the valley was always wrapped in _____.

14. The ship sent up a _____ to signal other vessels.

15. Julia always rides her red _____ to school.

16. Have you ever watched that _____ on how to exercise.

Home Involvement Activity Many products, such as health and beauty aids, have names that are clipped or blended words. How many of these words can you name? List them. Look in magazines or flyers for examples.

Name _____

Helpful Hint

Language is always changing. English borrows words from many other languages. Some words stay the same. Other words change a little. Here are some **borrowed words:**

lasso (from Spanish)   **pretzel** (from German)
karate (from Japanese)   **menu** (from French)

BIENVENUE EN
PARTIE FRANÇAISE
WELCOME TO
THE FRENCH SIDE

Each word in the box below has been borrowed from another language. On the line, write the word from the box that fits each clue.

aloha	garage	gymnastics	honcho	khaki	plaza
noodle	opossum	parka	piano	percent	coffee

1. French word for a place to keep a car _____

2. Aleut word for a hooded jacket _____

3. German word for a flat strip of dry dough, served in soup _____

4. Algonquian word for a small animal with a ratlike tail _____

5. Hawaiian word for *hello* and *good-by* _____

6. Arabic word for a dark-brown drink _____

7. Hindi word for a dull yellowish-brown color or cloth _____

8. Japanese word for the person in charge _____

9. Latin word meaning "a hundredth part" _____

10. Spanish word for a public square _____

11. Italian word for a musical instrument _____

12. Greek word for the sport of exercising _____

CHALLENGE

Match the name of each invention with the language it came from. Use a dictionary to help you.

robot   Latin
wheel   Czech
tractor   Greek

Solve this puzzle that uses borrowed words. Write one letter in each space. Then copy the letters in the shaded column, from top to bottom, to answer the question below. Each answer appears in the Word Bank, along with the language from which it was borrowed.

1. opening in a wall to let in light _ _ _ _ _ _

2. temporary house made of ice _ _ _ _ _

3. African trip for photographing animals _ _ _ _ _ _

4. fastener for clothes _ _ _ _ _ _

5. sparkling blue gemstone _ _ _ _ _ _ _ _

6. Hawaiian wreath of flowers _ _ _

7. pepper that makes a red spice _ _ _ _ _ _ _

8. highest singing voice _ _ _ _ _ _ _

9. something sticky you chew _ _ _

10. soap for washing your hair _ _ _ _ _ _ _

11. part of a story or series _ _ _ _ _ _ _

12. a food made from milk _ _ _ _ _ _

13. Western farm for horses _ _ _ _ _

14. glass showing your reflection _ _ _ _ _ _

15. popular red sauce for hamburgers _ _ _ _ _ _ _

16. wild animal like a thin, small wolf _ _ _ _ _ _

Question: What is so special about Barrow, Alaska?

Answer: It is the _____ in the United States.

Word Bank

Chinese: ketchup	*Greek:* episode	*Icelandic:* window	*Sanskrit:* sapphire
Egyptian: gum	*Hawaiian:* lei	*Italian:* soprano	*Spanish:* ranch
Eskimo: igloo	*Hindi:* shampoo	*Latin:* mirror	*Swahili:* safari
French: button	*Hungarian:* paprika	*Nahuatl:* coyote	*Turkish:* yogurt

LESSON 104: Borrowed Words

Home Involvement Activity Many food names, such as **ravioli, tortilla, sushi,** and **sauerkraut,** are borrowed from other languages. Work together to list foods that you eat whose names are borrowed words.

Name _____

Helpful Hint

An **eponym** is a word that came from the name of a person. English contains many eponyms. Each eponym has a story behind it. Here are two eponyms you may know:

sandwich—named after John Montagu, 4th Earl of Sandwich

Braille—named for Louis Braille, a French teacher who invented this system of printing and writing for the blind

A student learning **Braille**

Read the list of words or names in the box. Match each word with the clue that tells how the word got its name. Write the word from the box on the line. Use a dictionary, if needed.

| cardigan | Georgia | Pennsylvania | saxophone | silhouette |

1. _____ is one of the 13 original colonies.
   William Penn (1644–1718) founded the colony and gave it his name.

2. A _____ is an outline drawing cut from black paper.
   French leader Etienne de— (1709–1767) liked this cheap way to do portraits.

3. _____ is a Southern state and one of the 13 original colonies.
   This state was named after King George II of England, who gave money to make it a colony.

4. A _____ is a knitted sweater or jacket that buttons down the front.
   English general James Brudenell, 7th Earl of— (1797–1868), wore this style.

5. A _____ is a brass wind instrument with valves, from Belgium.
   Inventor Adolphe Sax made this musical instrument more than a century ago.

CHALLENGE

Many scientific words are eponyms. Use a dictionary to discover where the following names came from and what they mean:

**diesel   volt
hertz   curium**

Copyright © by William H. Sadlier, Inc. All rights reserved.

LESSON 105: Eponyms and Collective Nouns   **213**

The Milky Way **Galaxy**

Each phrase below contains a collective noun. Underline the group of people, animals, or things that are named in this way. Then write the word on the line.

1. a **deck** of _____   boats   cards   ducks

2. a **company** of _____   soldiers   water   geese

3. a **crew** of _____   tar   dogs   sailors

4. a **grove** of _____   trees   graves   tables

5. a **mound** of _____   air   teachers   dirt

6. a **herd** of _____   cattle   cars   violins

7. a **pride** of _____   mice   lions   babies

8. a **school** of _____   fish   books   grades

9. a **swarm** of _____   money   bees   sandwiches

10. a **fleet** of _____   checkers   ships   papers

Choose the collective noun from the box below that best completes each sentence. Write the word on the line.

committee	nest	troop	team

11. Have you seen the _____ of sparrows by the chimney?

12. You have to be at least eight years old to join a Scout _____.

13. The audience applauded the _____ of gymnasts.

14. A _____ of senators will vote on the issue of raising taxes.

Home Involvement Activity Work together to find out the history of these fashion words. For whom was each named: **mackintosh, Levi's, raglan sleeve, chesterfield?** Then clip and label an example of each from a catalog.

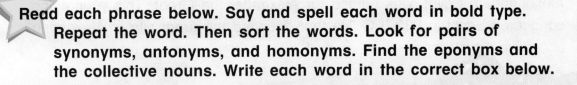

Name _____

Read each phrase below. Say and spell each word in bold type. Repeat the word. Then sort the words. Look for pairs of synonyms, antonyms, and homonyms. Find the eponyms and the collective nouns. Write each word in the correct box below.

- **sealing** a package
- **seldom** hear music
- wore a **cardigan**
- **often** eat pasta
- a **temporary** shelter
- repeat your **response**
- left a **permanent** stain
- play the **saxophone**
- an **accelerated** pace

- watch a **whale** in Alaska
- hear the wind **wail**
- cut out a **silhouette**
- the correct **answer**
- painting the **ceiling**
- take a **brisk** walk
- a **herd** of buffalo
- a **pride** of lions
- a **swarm** of bees

A humpback **whale** breaching

Synonyms	Antonyms	Homonyms

Eponyms	Collective Nouns

SPELL & WRITE

Many place names are eponyms. These places were named for the people who founded, conquered, or ruled them. For example, the city of Alexandria, in Egypt, was named for Alexander the Great. This young king conquered Egypt in 332 B.C. He then founded the great city of Alexandria and gave it his name.

With a small group of classmates, brainstorm a list of places, such as Alexandria, Pennsylvania, or New York, that were named after people. First, choose a place. Next, look in a print or an on-line encyclopedia to find out all that you can. Take notes. Then write a brief research report to explain how the place got its name. Use at least two of these spelling words.

sealing	seldom	cardigan	often	temporary	response
permanent	saxophone	accelerated	whale	wail	silhouette
answer	ceiling	brisk	herd	pride	swarm

Alexander the Great

Writer's Tip

State your topic in the **introduction.** Develop it in the **body** of your report. Summarize your information in the **conclusion.**

Speaker's Challenge

Present your report to the class. First, make an outline of your main points. Next, write your outline on note cards. Then, practice speaking from your cards. Use a strong voice.

Alexandria, Egypt, today

Name _____

> **Helpful Hint**

An **idiomatic expression** (or **idiom**) is a phrase that means something different from what it seems to mean. Idiomatic expressions are part of everyday speech.

Our dinner was **on the house.** *means* Our dinner was *free.*
I **hit it off** with her parents. *means* I *got along well* with her parents.
This lesson is **over his head.** *means* This lesson is *too hard for him.*

⭐ **Each numbered sentence has an idiom in bold type. Circle the letter of the answer that means the same thing.**

1. We decided to **clear the air.**
   a. We decided to drive only electric cars to reduce air pollution.
   b. We decided to buy room freshener to sweeten the air.
   c. We decided to say what was on our minds to get rid of the tension.

2. The science test was **a snap.**
   a. The science test was a surprise quiz.
   b. The science test was very easy.
   c. The science test was very hard.

3. I thought that the new movie was **for the birds.**
   a. I thought that the new movie was terrible.
   b. I thought that the new movie was about crows.
   c. I thought that the new movie had too much singing in it.

4. Cory's grade is **up in the air.**
   a. Cory's grade is an *A.*
   b. Cory's grade flew away.
   c. Cory's teacher has not yet decided Cory's grade.

Danny's Diner
GUEST CHECK
04847

Roast Fresh Turkey 16.95
Vegetable Platter 13.95
2 Iced Tea 4.50

FREE

$35.40
TAX 2.83
TOTAL: $38.23

> **CHALLENGE**

Draw a funny cartoon to illustrate one of these **idiomatic expressions** or another one you know. Ask a classmate to guess the idiom you have drawn.

Each sentence at the left has an idiom in bold type. Draw a line to match the sentence at the left with the sentence at the right that means the same thing.

1. They **put their heads together.**   a. They got the most attention.

2. They **talked my ear off.**   b. They thought about it together.

3. They **stole the spotlight.**   c. They chatted endlessly.

4. He's **up to his ears** in homework.   a. He is in trouble.

5. He **calls the shots.**   b. He is overwhelmed.

6. He's **in hot water.**   c. He is in charge.

7. We were still **in the running.**   a. We were running away from something.

8. We were **on the run.**   b. We had a chance to win the contest.

9. We were **running rings around** them.   c. We were beating them.

10. She was **hot under the collar.**   a. She felt very angry.

11. She could not make **head or tail of** it.   b. She realized what might happen.

12. She saw **the handwriting on the wall.**   c. She could not understand.

Choose four idioms from above. Write a sentence for each one.

13. _____

_____

14. _____

_____

15. _____

_____

16. _____

_____

Home Involvement Activity Have family members write down idioms they use. Then have other family members define the idioms. If someone in your family speaks another language, have that person share some amusing idioms.

Name _____

Analogy questions often appear on standardized tests. **Word analogies** test your ability to understand how words and ideas relate. Read this:

Up is to **down** as **fast** is to **slow**.

THINK: Up and **down** are *opposites*. **Fast** and **slow** are *opposites*.

The words in both pairs relate in exactly the same way.
Both are **antonyms.**

You can also write the analogy like this: **up : down :: fast : slow**

Here are some other ways that pairs of words and ideas are related:

They are *synonyms*.	**Fix** is to **repair** as **sew** is to **mend.**
They show *cause and effect*.	**Tired** is to **rest** as **happy** is to **smile.**
They show *parts of a whole*.	**room : house :: page : book**
They show *how objects are used*.	**pen : write :: crayon : draw**
They show *how products are produced.*	**milk : cow :: honey : bee**

Read each word analogy. Write the correct description from the box below to show how the words in both pairs are related. The first answer is given.

word : antonym	object : use	product : producer
word : synonym	cause : effect	part : whole

1. *Axe* is to *chop* as *scissors* is to *cut*.   **object : use**

2. *Toe* is to *foot* as *branch* is to *tree*. _____

3. *Heat* is to *melt* as *cold* is to *freeze*. _____

4. *Top* is to *bottom* as *left* is to *right*. _____

5. cheese : goat :: feathers : chicken _____

6. fast : speedy :: heavy : weighty _____

7. knife : slice :: strainer : drain _____

8. tall : short :: narrow : wide _____

CHALLENGE

Make up three word analogies. Leave out the last word in each. Challenge a classmate to complete your analogies.

Circle the letter of the word that completes each analogy. Then write the word on the line.

1. *Foot* is to *leg* as *mouth*

   is to _____.
   a. teeth
   b. lips
   c. ear
   d. face

2. *Rope* is to *mountain climbing* as *racket*

   is to _____.
   a. football
   b. volleyball
   c. tennis
   d. ice hockey

3. *Bat* is to *hit* as *glove*

   is to _____.
   a. mitten
   b. buy
   c. uniform
   d. catch

4. *Hungry* is to *eat* as *study*

   is to _____.
   a. student
   b. learn
   c. write
   d. lesson

5. *Easy* is to *simple* as *hard*

   is to _____.
   a. difficult
   b. harder
   c. soft
   d. rock

6. *Book* is to *library* as *dish*

   is to _____.
   a. eating
   b. silverware
   c. dinner
   d. cupboard

7. Bad : good ::

   fat :_____.
   a. thin
   b. eat
   c. hungry
   d. pork

8. thin : slender ::

   injury : _____.
   a. thick
   b. wound
   c. slim
   d. doctor

9. Wool : sheep ::

   feathers : _____.
   a. fur
   b. goose
   c. cotton
   d. whale

10. tickle : giggle ::

    embarrass : _____.
    a. run
    b. blush
    c. laugh
    d. smile

Home Involvement Activity Solve this word analogy: *Composer* is to *symphony* as *carpenter* is to _____. Explain your answer. Make up other analogies to solve together.

Name _____

⭐ **Read about the dazzling northern lights that you can sometimes see in Alaska's night sky. Then answer the questions that follow.**

Fire in the Sky

by David Foster

It's a shivering-cold night in Alaska—a good night to stay in by the fire. So why are people standing outside in the snow, hooting and hollering? Follow their gaze upward and you'll see. Ghostly, glowing ribbons of green, white, blue, and red are moving across the sky. It's the best fireworks show in the sky—the northern lights.

The northern lights' shimmering dance has mystified people for thousands of years. Ancient Eskimos believed the lights were spirits playing ball with a walrus head. Some gold-rush prospectors thought the lights were vapors rising from a hidden mine.

Today's scientists are more factual. They say the northern lights, also called the *aurora borealis,* occur when tiny particles from the sun hit Earth's atmosphere. The sun gives off not only heat and light but solar wind—a stream of electrically charged atomic particles. As they approach Earth, the particles are guided by our planet's magnetic field toward the North and South poles. Sixty to 200 miles above the ground, the particles collide with air molecules and make them glow like a neon sign.

Sometimes the aurora is a broad sheet of light. At other times, it looks like wavy ribbons. Big displays can last hours, with rays of light darting across the sky 100 times faster than a jet airplane! They also make a crackling noise.

Usually the northern lights appear only in the Far North. But sometimes solar flares whip up big magnetic storms around Earth and create auroras that spread farther south. These rare southern appearances can cause quite a stir!

🏛 Reader's Response

1. **What are some stories that people have made up about the northern lights?**

2. **How do scientists explain the northern lights?**

3. **If you were looking at the northern lights, how do you think you would feel?**

For thousands of years, the people in what is now Alaska have been watching the dazzling displays of the northern lights. As with other natural events, ancient peoples made up stories to try to explain this grand fireworks display. Today, scientists know that the appearance of the northern lights is based on solar activity. Yet the old myths still entertain us.

Make up your own myth about the northern lights. You could begin by reading some "how" or "why" stories. Native American myths are filled with stories that explain *how* or *why* something happens in nature. Then write your own myth. Explain why the northern lights occur. Use your imagination. Include at least two of these words.

> beginning   later   meanwhile   now   when   while   therefore   but   yet
> before   after   although   create   observe   first   next   then   finally

---

_____

_____

_____

_____

_____

_____

_____

_____

_____

_____

Writer's Tips

- Include a strong sequence of events in your myth.

- Use transition words, such as *first, next,* and *then,* to connect your ideas and make them flow.

Writer's Challenge

Use science and facts to explain why another natural event occurs. For example, tell why earthquakes happen. Do some research. Then write a paragraph to explain this natural event.

The northern lights in Alaska

LESSON 109: Connecting Reading and Writing Comprehension—Distinguish Between Fact and Fiction; Synthesize

Name _____

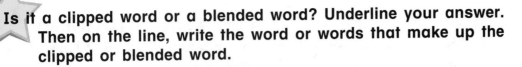

★ **Is it a clipped word or a blended word? Underline your answer. Then on the line, write the word or words that make up the clipped or blended word.**

1. gas   clipped word   blended word   _____

2. telethon   clipped word   blended word   _____

3. champ   clipped word   blended word   _____

4. smog   clipped word   blended word   _____

5. grad   clipped word   blended word   _____

6. moped   clipped word   blended word   _____

7. flu   clipped word   blended word   _____

8. brunch   clipped word   blended word   _____

★ **Each sentence below has an idiom in bold type. Circle the letter of the answer that means the same thing.**

9. Our dinner was **on the house.**
   a. Our dinner tasted like wallpaper paste.
   b. Our dinner was free.
   c. Our dinner came from an old family recipe.

10. We are **in hot water.**
    a. We are all old sailors.
    b. We are going to take a bath.
    c. We are in big trouble.

★ **Circle the letter of the word that best completes each analogy. Then write the word on the line.**

11. Sleepy : yawn :: unhappy : _____
    a. happy
    b. frown
    c. laugh
    d. gloomy

12. Much : little :: late : _____
    a. soon
    b. morning
    c. few
    d. early

Read the passage. Then circle the letter of the answers below.

Fairbanks, Alaska, hosts the World Eskimo-Indian Olympics (<u>WEIO</u>) each year. Contestants come from all over the <u>state</u>. Each year sees record-breaking crowds and more participants than the year before.

The events at the WEIO are not like those you may know. Yet all WEIO events have a common origin. They test the strength, agility, balance, and endurance needed to live in the <u>harsh</u> climate of the frozen north. The competitors show survival skills in events such as the knuckle hop, kneel jump, stick pull, ear weight, one-hand reach, and toe kick.

The blanket toss, or *nalakatuk,* is a popular WEIO event. It echoes a survival skill—the ability to spot game far off in the distance. The blanket is a walrus skin. A group of people hold it and stretch it like a trampoline. One person gets on the skin. That person gets <u>tossed</u> into the air. Judges look for the best height, balance, and air movements.

1. **WEIO** is the abbreviation for
   a. World Eskimo-Inuit Olympics.
   b. Weight Endurance International Open.
   c. World Eskimo-Indian Olympics.
   d. World Eskimo International Olympics.

2. You will find the word **state** on a dictionary page with the guide words
   a. staple – startle.
   b. starve – station.
   c. statue – steady.
   d. standard – star.

3. The best *antonym* for **harsh** is
   a. gentle.   b. changing.
   c. severe.   d. cool.

4. A *synonym* for **tossed** is
   a. thrown.   b. waved.
   c. caught.   d. lowered.

Extend & Apply

Visit the Web site at **www.weio.org** to find out more about the blanket toss and other events at the WEIO Olympics. Which do you think would be the most fun to see?